Decline of the Superpowers

Winners and Losers in
Today's Global Economy

Decline of the $uper-powers

JAMES LAXER

James Lorimer & Company, Publishers
Toronto, 1987

Cover design: Don Fernley

Canadian Cataloguing in Publication Data

Laxer, James, 1941-
 Decline of the Superpowers

ISBN 0-88862-893-5 (bound). -ISBN 0-88862-892-7 (pbk.)

1. Economic history -1945 - . 2. Economic Policy.
I. Title.

HC59.L39 1987   330.9'04   C87-094466-5

James Lorimer & Company, Publishers
Egerton Ryerson Memorial Building
35 Britain Street
Toronto, Ontario M5A 1R7

Printed and Bound in Canada

5 4 3 2 1 87 88 89 90 91

To my neighbours in Beaumont du Ventoux

Contents

Acknowledgments

The writing of this book owes a great deal to a number of people. To Professor S.O. Kjellberg, I express gratitude for his stimulating intellectual companionship and advice. I owe my appreciation to Professor David Davies, former chairperson of the Political Science Department at Atkinson College, York University, and Professor Ron Bordessa, former dean of Atkinson College, for their administrative efforts which have made possible the studies over the last three years that have led to this book.

Without the efforts of many people working for and with the National Film Board of Canada, this book would not have been possible. Their participation in the *Reckoning* film series, in which I was involved, gave me an extraordinary opportunity to look directly at the economies of the leading industrial countries. To name some of those involved, I wish to thank John Taylor, Erna Buffie, Colleen Bostwick, Kalle Lasn, Jefferson Lewis, Bob Lower, Kent Martin, Tom Shandel and Moira Simpson for the privilege of our mutual collaboration.

To Curtis Fahey, who encouraged me in the writing of this book from across the Atlantic Ocean and who offered an invaluable editorial critique, I offer my thanks.

My wife, Sandy, shared the adventure of living in Beaumont du Ventoux, France, where this book took shape. Without her understanding, *Decline of the Superpowers* would not have been written.

James Laxer, Beaumont du Ventoux, France, June 1987.

Introduction

Taking Stock of a Revolution

A global economic revolution is underway in the late 20th century. Its dramatic effects are being widely felt, although the revolution is far from well understood in the English-speaking world. The signposts of the revolution are there for everyone to witness.

- On the slopes of Japan's holy Mount Fuji, near ancient Buddhist temples, sounds the eerie hum of factories in which robots produce other robots, seven days a week, twenty-four hours a day. In the more prosaic setting of a Mitsubishi showroom in Tokyo, businessmen are learning about production robots they can rent to improve the efficiency of their companies.

- In San Diego, California, Sony operates a television assembly plant where the workers' wages are 15 per cent less than they would be in Japan.[1] In many cases now, Japanese companies are opening plants in the United States not merely to get behind the wall of American protectionism but to avail themselves of labour costs which are lower in the United States than at home.

- In the autumn of 1986, a study published in the *Harvard Business Review* concluded that, despite the fact that production robots were an American invention, the Japanese showed greater "technological literacy" in their use. "Rather than narrowing the competitive gap with Japan, the technology of automation is widening it further," the study concluded.[2]

- In the city of Toulouse on the arid plateau near the Spanish border, French workers produce jet aircraft for Arbus Industrie Limited, a western European consortium which has successfully challenged the great American aircraft manufacturers and is now planning to produce its own jumbo jet for the turn-of-the-century international market.

- In the Gare de Lyon, the Parisian train station that still has overtones of the belle époque, waits the orange electric passenger train, the TGV, which is about to whisk its passengers to Marseilles in five hours at a cruising speed of 270 kilometers an hour — the fastest train in the world.

- In the hills of Manchester, England, where the first industrial revolution began two centuries ago, the air is clear — the textile mills have shut their doors and the industry that made England the workshop of the world is now centred in Asia.

Behind the visible signs are potent changes in the global economic order:

- For forty years, from the end of the Second World War to the mid-1980s, the United States has had a rate of productivity growth less than that of Japan, West Germany, France and Italy.

- Since 1973 there has been no increase in the standard of living of the average American.

- In the autumn of 1986, Japan's per capita income pulled even with that in the United States. The same is almost certain to occur in the leading Western European countries in the next few years. When it happens the per capita income of the major English-speaking countries — the United States, Britain and Canada — will have fallen below that of their leading competitors in East Asia and Western Europe.

In the late 20th century, people are on the lookout for revolutions, though often in the wrong places. The revolutions they anticipate do not occur, while all around them, unexpected revolutions unfold. The decline of America since the Second World War, in favour not of a rising Soviet empire or the Third World, but of advanced capitalism in east Asia and Western Europe, is the great geo-political revolution of our times.

How has all this occurred? How did the United States, uniquely positioned to dominate the global economy in 1945, lose out to those who lost the war? How did economic thinking in the English-speaking world get so out of touch with reality that these momentous changes are hardly perceived, let alone understood? How has the technological revolution of the past decade affected all of this?

Two momentous transitions have occurred in the global economy in the mid-1980s. The crucial event of 1985 was the emergence of the United States as a net debtor nation. This development was historic, for the United States had been a net creditor nation since the end of the First World War. To illustrate just how large a shift has occurred, consider this: in 1967, the United States was a net creditor to the extent of 9 per cent of its Gross National Product (GNP). If present trends continue, by 1990, the U.S. could become a net debtor to the tune of 16 per cent of its GNP or close to one trillion dollars. In the 1980s, dependence of borrowers in U.S. credit markets on foreign investors has grown enormously to $110 billion in 1986 alone, nearly double the borrowing in 1985 of $59 billion which in turn was more than double the 1983 level.[3] U.S. Federal Reserve Chairman, Paul A. Volcker, worried about the potential American vulnerability this created, made the following comment in testimony before the American Congress in November 1986: "We are now by far the world's largest debtor country, and even under favourable circumstances that net indebtedness will increase substantially further in the years ahead.... In the more immediate future the relevant question is whether foreigners will remain so willing to employ so large a fraction of their savings in our markets."[4]

The great economic event of 1986 concerned the opposite side of the coin — Japan's replacement of the United States as the most important banker to the world. In recent years, a torrent of Japanese capital has been flowing into the United States. In 1982, the net capital flow from Japan to the United States was 1.7 billion dollars; in 1983, 5.5 billion dollars; in 1984, 14.8 billion; and in 1985, 33.16 billion dollars. Japan's role as a financial power involved both the lending of Japanese capital to governments and enterprises around the world, and the growth of direct Japanese foreign investments through the opening of branch plants in many countries including the United States. Moreover, in 1986 the 40 per cent appreciation of the yen against the U.S. dollar caused an enormous growth in the value of Japanese savings available for investment abroad. Before the increase in the value of the yen, Japanese foreign assets had been increasing at a rate of 28 per cent a year.[5] The high yen meant that Japanese foreign investment could expand at an even faster rate. Japan's career as an economic superpower was only beginning.

The world has also grown used to enormous Japanese surpluses in merchandise trade. In 1985, Japan scored a $50 billion surplus in trade, while the United States suffered a trade deficit of $150 billion. These Japanese trade surpluses and American deficits indicated that the American edge in industrial production in key commodities had ended. When it came to the efficient production of automobiles, electronic equipment and machine tools, the Japanese were clearly second to none. Originally, Americans bought Japanese goods to save money; now they did so because they represented the best quality.

The rise of Japan to the status of international banker, foreign investor and industrial power ought to be familiar to Americans. After all, this is what happened to the United States in the golden years of American foreign investment — the decades following the Second World War. American manufacturing strength, then out of reach of any other nation, provided the underpinning for U.S. investments in many parts of the globe. It appeared for a considerable time that what was occurring was a virtual Americanization of the rest of the world.

At the beginning of the 1960s, America was supreme in the world. When they went abroad, Americans knew that they came from a country that was vastly wealthier than any other. When they compared their living standards to those of other people, they rightly felt that they lived in a world apart. In 1960, Americans were already enjoying full-blown mass consumption. Automobiles, television sets, telephones, refrigerators, washers and dryers existed in abundance. Americans were well housed and well fed. American industry, anchored on the prodigious output of the northeast and midwest, was superior to anything in the world. In those days, people marvelled at the great Ford plant just outside Detroit as a kind of "eighth industrial wonder of the world." Across South Chicago sprawled the centre of the world's steel industry and in 1960 nations still regarded steel output as the key measure of industrial might. In terms of sheer economic clout, the United States loomed over the other nations of the capitalist world like a colossus. Its Gross Domestic Product (GDP) was greater than the combined economic output of the next six non-communist countries — Japan, West Germany, the United Kingdom, France, Italy and Canada. The extent to which U.S. output exceeded that of all the others, 15 per cent, was greater than the total output of the British economy.[6]

In such a world, it was no wonder that millions looked to the United States, almost as to another planet inhabited by supermen, for economic, political and military leadership. They looked as well to America for hope, for their own dreams of mass consumption. For ordinary people in other countries, America was a land of milk and honey. For political leaders, it was a centre of unimaginable power. American leaders were able to make global decisions with an ease that would have confounded the rulers of all the great empires of the past.

But in the quarter-century that followed 1960, the colossus stumbled. By the mid-1980s, the United States had been reduced to merely human proportions. It was still by far the largest power in the world. But it had lost its industrial supremacy, it was losing its edge as banker to the world, and its status as the greatest foreign investor on earth was fast eroding. Perhaps most important of all, the United States failed to deliver the goods to its own people, while other industrial countries were much more successful. The gap in material lifestyle between Americans and people in the other leading industrial countries was closing quickly.

Let us illustrate America's decline with the use of one very broad and significant measure: the increase in real Gross Domestic Product (GDP) per capita. This tells us how much the real income of a country per person has increased year by year. From 1960 to 1984, America's real per capita GDP grew by an average of 2.1 per cent a year, and virtually all of this increase occurred between 1960 and 1973. In Japan the increase in per capita GDP for the same period was 5.8 per cent per year, in France and Italy 3.2 per cent, in West Germany 2.7 per cent, and in Canada 2.8 per cent. Only Britain, with an increase in per capita GDP of 1.9 per cent per year, did worse among the major industrialized countries.[7]

What did this mean for the living standard of average Americans? The American dream had always been based on the idea that each generation of Americans would end up better off than its predecessors. By the mid-1980s, that promise was wearing thin. Since 1973, average weekly earnings in the United States have declined by 14.3 per cent after accounting for inflation. In addition, median household income in the U.S. dipped about 6 per cent from 1973 to the mid-1980s. Real hourly earnings in manufacturing in the United States did not increase at all between 1973 and 1979 and fell by an average of .8 per cent per year from 1979 to 1984. While in 1973 the earnings of an average thirty-year-old American had been $23,580 a year (in 1984 dollars), by 1984, the average had dropped steeply to $17,520, not much above the 1959 figure — $17,188 (in 1984 dollars).[8]

The revolution in comparative international living standards was accompanied by a very large shift in the overall weight of the economies concerned. In 1960 the American economy produced nearly five times the output of Japan, the second largest non-communist economy, but by 1986 Japan's total output of goods and services was half of that of the U.S. Taken together, the next six industrial economies in 1986 had a total output approximately 30 per cent larger than that of the United States instead of the U.S. outproducing them all as in 1960.[9]

Important shifts had also taken place in the ranks of major industrial rivals of the United States. The most dramatic change, of course, involved Japan, which by the mid-1980s had become an economic superpower in its own right. In terms of overall economic weight it had pulled away from the rest of the six, leaving West Germany a very distant third with a GDP only half of that of Japan. In 1960, West Germany's GDP had equalled 70 per cent of Japan's.[10] In addition, France and Italy had gained weight in relation to West Germany, while Britain had lost weight. In absolute terms, Britain's economy had been larger than France's in 1960. By the mid-1980s, France had sped ahead of Britain in both total GDP and per capita income and Italy had virtually caught up with Britain in per capita income.[11]

It was exceptionally difficult for Americans to understand that their power in the world was diminishing. It is, in general, hard for dominant nations to have a clear perspective of their place in the world. But there are particular reasons why it has been even more difficult for Americans.

One reason is that the late 20th century is the age of faddish, ephemeral change. The media announce stunning changes all the time in the style of things, in the personalities who have power or are losing it. Surrounded by the pyrotechnics of dramatic "change" in the daily news and dulled by the conventional wisdom that modern society is characterized by change, really fundamental transformations become all the harder to observe.

Related to the problem of the way the media trumpets minor change and makes basic change hard to see, is the narrowing effect media reporting of international affairs has on the way Americans perceive their country's economic position. Americans are world-wise enough to know that not so many centuries ago the Chinese thought of their country as the "middle kingdom," portraying it on maps of the world in the very centre, with only a few unimportant territories floating around the periphery. This has become the famous symbol of a people so self-absorbed that they have no perspective on the wider world. In the late 20th century Americans are not so far from thinking of their country as the "middle kingdom." True, the American media bring them in daily electronic contact with the rest of the world — but on a highly selective basis. Almost all news reported in the United States has to do with the world as it affects Americans. Vietnam, Iran, Nicaragua, the middle east, terrorism in Europe have all been seen this way. The cumulative effect is that, while Americans may imagine that they are in touch with the world, in reality they are focusing almost entirely on the question of "trouble spots" for the United States and Americans. Almost nothing external to the United States is seen or understood for its own sake.

Post-War System in Crisis

Much more has happened than that the fortunes of some countries have risen while the fortunes of others have fallen. Competitive success and failure among nations are not isolated phenomena. They are the result of interactions within the international economic order. And the global economic system no longer functions as it was designed to in the post-war period. Since the early 1970s, the system has tottered from crisis to crisis, with no resolution of its basic problems; and since the sharp recession of the early 1980s, none of the major industrial nations has achieved a high rate of growth for any sustained period.

The international economic system established at the end of the Second World War was explicitly based on the supremacy of the United States, its institutional framework premised on the durability of American superiority. In 1945, the United States enjoyed a unique opportunity to reshape the world — or rather the very large part of it in which it was dominant — in its own image. That opportunity was greatest in the defeated countries — Japan, Western Germany, and Italy — but it was also very considerable in the countries that had been America's allies — Britain, France and Canada. Never in history had one power had such an opportunity to wipe the slate of human affairs clean and to declare a new beginning as the United States had in 1945.

Only the Soviet Union and the countries which became its satellites, managed to stay outside the orbit of the United States. (Later in this book, we will analyse how the alternative Soviet system has fared in competition with the leading industrial powers of the capitalist world.)

The institutional framework for the post-war international economy was simple enough: the key creations were the International Monetary Fund (IMF), the World Bank and the General Agreement on Tariffs and Trade (GATT). But what gave life to the system was a vision of how a prosperous economic order could be achieved — and that vision was American, a product of American history and thinking. The American idea of the post-war world flowed naturally from the experience and thought of the United States and from the uniquely advantageous position of the country. The new international economic order was to be based on the ideal of a global free-market economy, in which the barriers to trade and to the free flow of investment among nations would be progressively rolled back. Free trade and the right of investment anywhere might take a long time to achieve in a complete form, but they were ideals to which the world could aspire.

American motives in sponsoring such an economic order were mixed, a complex combination of self-interest and idealism. It is not hard, in retrospect, to see the self-interest. At the end of the war, half the goods and services on the globe were being produced in the United States. For such a country, it was hard to imagine that free trade and the free flow of investment could ever be anything but beneficial. But along with self-interest, there was a powerful strain of American idealism which held that all humanity could benefit from the 'truths' history had taught Americans about the ordering of economies and societies. If, as many believed at the end of the conflict, the war had been caused by the pursuit of narrow national self-interest by competing states, then the road to peace as well as to prosperity surely lay in the building of a new order found on the general principles of a market economy open to all.

The first steps toward setting up the post-war economic system were taken while the war was still being fought, in the unlikely setting of rural New Hampshire, at Bretton Woods, in the summer of 1944. At Bretton Woods, the Americans and their allies agreed that a cornerstone of the post-war economic order would be a system of fixed exchange rates for currencies, with the U.S. dollar as the reserve currency, the anchor of the system — a currency into which any other would be convertible, an instrument through which all international obligations could be met. The U.S. dollar would be as good as gold, convertible into gold at $35 an ounce. Not everyone at Bretton Woods was happy with this decision. John Maynard Keynes, who represented Britain there, had preferred to see a new international reserve currency created, rather than giving the U.S. dollar this role. His proposal was intended to limit American power to control international credit, and was therefore, in his view, in the interest of debtor nations such as Britain. At Bretton Woods, however, it was the Americans who held the cards.

The Bretton Woods conference created both the IMF and the World Bank. The IMF was set up to assure liquidity in international commerce. It was to provide loans to nations experiencing balance of payments difficulties, as long as those nations undertook to conduct their affairs in keeping with the principles of an open-market system. From the beginning, the IMF was to be an instrument of American power, a means by which the United States, as the country providing the liquidity, could insist on the rebuilding of other nations along lines acceptable to it. The World Bank, formally called the International Bank for Reconstruction and Development (IBRD), was founded in response to a call for development aid to weaker countries, particularly those whose economies had been devastated by the war. The original notion — that of Keynes — was to establish a bank that would provide credit on a very large scale, and not according to strict commercial principles, for the development of economically backward countries. The concern was for the creation of an international economic system in which balanced trade between more or less equal players would be possible, instead of an unequal contest between developed and underdeveloped nations. Despite these far-reaching aims, the World Bank ended up being a very conservative institution, whose governing body reflected economic power rather than the principle of direct democratic control by all the nations involved. The World Bank provided loans on strict commercial terms, punishing countries with a history of loan defaults. Although later in its history it was to provide some capital on a non-commercial basis, the World Bank operated on principles similar to xx Decline of the Superpowers

those of the IMF and, with its perennial American presidents, became very much a tool of U.S. power.

GATT, not set up until 1948, was to coordinate the move toward freer trade internationally. With a broad mandate to promote non-discriminatory trade relations, GATT's job was to oversee the even-handed removal of tariff barriers between nations. Later, by the 1970s, when tariffs had fallen substantially, the organization would become embroiled in the much more difficult task of wrestling with non-tariff barriers — all the measures used by states to promote domestic industrial development which could have an impact on international trade.

The American post-war vision was perhaps more elegant than the result. The enormous power imbalance between the United States and other nations in the early post-war years meant that the system could not work as intended for a considerable period. Many countries were forced to maintain foreign exchange controls until the end of the 1950s and serious multilateral efforts toward freer trade did not get underway until the 1960s.

The insistence on making the dollar the international reserve currency flowed from the sense Americans had of their country's unchallengeable strength. It was to mean, for example, that the United States could run a balance of payments deficit for long periods without having to settle its accounts. What was not perceived so clearly at the outset was that for the system to work, to be liquid, the United States actually needed to run a virtually continuous balance of payments deficit. This was because the system depended on the export of vast sums of American capital, both public and private. In the late 1940s, the public capital came via the Marshall Plan, Washington's fund for the rebuilding of Western Europe. Later, and in much greater amounts, public capital came from American military spending in other countries. At the same time, private capital was also flowing abroad as American companies took over foreign enterprises or set up branch plants as their way into markets abroad. The result of these massive exports of public and private capital was a perennial balance of payments deficit against the rest of the world. In the first post-war years, this deficit did not appear to matter much, since U.S. supremacy was so great. More than that, the deficit was essential to the functioning of the international system. Without it the international economy would have been starved of liquidity.

If there was to be a country with a structural deficit at the centre of the system, there would, of course, have to be countries with structural surpluses as well. The most successful of these were to become West Germany and Japan, countries whose economies would be designed precisely around exports. From the early 1950s, West Germany was to have a long string of current account surpluses and, by the end of the 1950s, Japan was in a position to do the same thing, on a much vaster scale. West Germany and Japan would receive foreign capital as well as generating their own. This, along with the fact that their own currencies were undervalued and that their industries paid low wages, would allow them to fashion economies that became mighty export machines.

Yet, for a long time, it appeared that American multinational investment was taking over the world. The whole world, or at least the capitalist world, was being Americanized. What was not noticed was that from the very beginning American general economic growth rates, and more important, productivity growth rates, lagged behind those of competitors. The problem was that the system virtually guaranteed a higher rate of industrial investment in countries such as West Germany and Japan than in the United States. No one, least of all the Americans, was concerned about this since the U.S. advantage at the start was so great. In the end, however, just as a steady trickle of water will one day fill a huge reservoir, it was to have enormous results. The nations that were seen as satellite industrial countries would ultimately be satellites no longer. They would equal and surpass the United States in productive capacities and the American-designed world would enter an era of crisis.

By the end of the 1950s, a few people had noticed that the United States no longer had enough gold to cover all the U.S. dollars held abroad. At the time, this was a matter for academic probing, not for political concern. In the next decade things were different. The juxtaposition of the Vietnam War with the maturing of the economies in Western Europe and Japan brought real change. Automobiles, electrical products and machinery poured into the American market from abroad. At the beginning of the 1970s, mounting balance of payments deficits led to crisis. In August 1971, the Nixon administration began to dismantle the economic order that had been constructed at Bretton Woods. Richard Nixon took the U.S. off the gold standard, leaving foreign central banks holding vast sums no longer backed in gold. Two years and two devaluations of the U.S. dollar later, the system of fixed exchange rates was abandoned in favour of the new system of floating exchange rates. The U.S. dollar had lost its supreme position as the reserve currency of the capitalist world.

The American dollar was at the centre of the misfortunes of the post-war economic system. In the late 1940s, the dollar was a problem because it was too strong and there were simply not enough dollars to allow the countries that were rebuilding from the war to buy what they desperately needed from the United States. By the early 1970s, the problem was too many dollars in the system, held by foreign central bankers. The dollar scarcity at the outset made the system unworkable without deliberate efforts by Washington to pump capital out to the world; and the dollar surplus in the seventies brought the system down. The first circumstance was a reflection of a too massive American economic superiority to allow for normal commercial relations; and the second circumstance reflected American competitive weakness at a time when no one had given a thought to how the world could operate without American dominance.

The questions that are central to our inquiry are as follows: why did the countries which were the major winners of the Second World War experience slower economic growth than their major competitors in the four decades that followed the war; why did the Soviet Union fail to mount an effective economic challenge to the leading industrial powers of the capitalist world; why did France, Italy, West Germany and Japan achieve the most rapid growth in the industrial world from the early post-war years to the 1980s? Naturally, our inquiry centres on the fortunes of the United States, the world's most important economic power, around which the global economic system has operated. In this book, we will survey the economic strategy of the United States and of the other major industrial countries to account for their different degrees of success.

This book will examine countries with three kinds of economic systems: "enterprise"; "command"; and "enterprise-intervention." The United States, Britain and Canada have operated enterprise economies — market-centred economies in which the private sector has been central and in which sustained intervention on the part of the state to set goals and to coordinate economic activity has been largely absent. The Soviet Union has had a command economy — a non-market system in which production proceeds on the basis of official directives conceived at the level of the political leadership and the top levels of the state bureaucracy. Japan, West Germany, France, Italy and Sweden have all operated enterprise-intervention economies where the private sector and the state have acted as partners, planning for long-term development, setting targets for technological breakthroughs, within the context of a market system.

We will discover that the countries with enterprise-intervention economies have achieved the greatest success. In analysing all three kinds of economies, we will try to account for this fact. We begin with a hypothesis: the enterprise-intervention economies have been better at planning for long-term technological advances and at achieving a working consensus among the major elements in their societies than have the other two systems. This is decidedly not the accepted view among Americans and people in other English-speaking countries, where the virtues of private enterprise and the market, and the evils of state intervention, have been raised almost to the status of a religion. In the United States it is axiomatic that economic efficiency is best promoted by getting the state off the back of the private sector. Let the private sector do the job of wealth creation and, in this way, the greatest efficiency will be realized, the theory goes. And yet, for the past four decades the historical experience has contradicted this notion, suggesting that Americans may not be able to become competitive again until they rethink their most central economic idea. Indeed, to overcome their problems, Americans have been redoubling their efforts to rid their economy of any elements of intervention in it, heading exactly in the opposite direction to that taken by their most formidable competitors.

By the early 1970s, as already noted, the American-designed international economic system entered a period of crisis. Since the major recession of 1981-82, that crisis has deepened and none of the major industrial powers has succeeded in achieving a sustained high rate of growth. We will examine the reasons for the crisis and speculate about the prospects for the international economic system being successfully reformed. In the next chapter, we will see how the Reagan administration and American conservatives tried to set things right in the 1980s by reasserting American leadership over the global economy. In subsequent chapters, we will examine the strategies pursued by America's competitors.

This book takes a comparative-historical approach, treating developments within each country as part of a process, and comparing the results in one case to results elsewhere. Economists often disparage such an approach, labelling it unscientific. What they fail to see is that this kind of subject cannot be successfully reduced to sets of numbers and equations, because we are discussing the social relationships among key groups of decision-makers as well as looking at the strategy of the state in one system as opposed to another. The advantage of the comparative-historical approach is that it helps get us around the reductionist argument that we can never really prove that one system has worked best, because we cannot know how well a country would have done had it tried another system. By examining a large number of cases in widely differing settings over a sustained period of time, we avoid a conundrum which so often stops economists from drawing conclusions on this subject.

Chapter One

How the Reagan Revolution Turned Out

By the end of the 1970s, Americans were acutely aware of their country's unaccustomed weakness in the world. American weakness was symbolized by Watergate, the fall of Saigon in 1975, the Iran hostage crisis, the flood of Japanese and West German goods into the U.S. market and the Soviet invasion of Afghanistan.

Well before the election of Ronald Reagan as President of the United States in November 1980, a resurgent conservative movement had articulated the basis on which American power could be restored. What was to become the "Reagan revolution" was a program for the reassertion of American military and economic power — in sum, of the global leadership of the United States. The conservative program was premised on two assumptions: that Soviet power posed the major threat to the American world position and that the revitalization of the American economy required the maximum possible limitation of state intervention in favour of a strengthened market economy. In the case of the economic program, while there were important differences among conservatives on questions such as the government deficit, there was no disagreement at all on the basic premise. The stronger the private sector, the theory was, the stronger would be the performance of the economy in terms of per capita income, productivity and general growth.

Nowhere were the premises of the Reagan revolution more clearly presented than in David Stockman's lament, *The Triumph of Politics*.[1] Stockman, the Budget Director of the Reagan administration until he quit in disgust in 1985 to write his exposé, summarized the conservative program as follows:

- a massive tax rollback.

- huge cuts in the non-military budget of the United States, accompanied by economic deregulation.

- a big boost to the defence budget.

The assumptions underlying the program were presented by Stockman with stunning simplicity. The tax cut would take billions of dollars away from government and put them in the hands of investors and consumers who would make the economy boom again. Budget cuts would achieve two desirable ends: the lancing of the bloated welfare state, and the termination of programs aimed at supporting various industrial and regional interests. (For Stockman, the idea that any state-operated industrial policy could improve on the performance of the market is an absurdity. In his view, all such policies are merely exercises in pork barrelling for politicians, with no potential for doing the economy any good.) In the case of the proposed increase in the defence budget, Stockman appears to have gone along with this aspect of the conservative program simply because it was a given of Reaganism, rather than as a matter of basic conviction.[2]

On the economic implications of the program, there was indeed an important element of disagreement among conservative thinkers which divided the monetarists from the supply-siders — Jude Wanniski, Arthur Laffer and Jack Kemp — who believed that you could cut taxes and raise the defence budget without causing a huge increase in the federal government's budgetary deficit. The supply- siders were confident that the tax cut would promote so much additional economic growth that it would generate enough extra tax revenue, at the lower tax rates, to prevent any revenue shortfall from emerging. The monetarists did not share this cheery faith. Their principal concern was to squeeze inflation out of the economy and their recipe for achieving this goal was to limit the growth of the money supply. The monetarists believed in classical capitalism, in an economic system in which government spending was severely checked and in which the state rejected the notion of a counter-cyclical fiscal policy. Severely limiting the macro-economic activity of the state would, they claimed, give the private sector the room to pursue non-inflationary, real growth, in which productive jobs would be created, as opposed to the make-work projects set up by government. The monetarists, whose chief apostle was Milton Friedman, provided neo-conservatism, the broad movement for a return to the basic tenets of American capitalism, with its intellectual muscle.

Even though Stockman considered himself a supply-sider, he shared the monetarist view that tax cuts alone would not suffice.[3] He argued that the only way to avoid a huge budget deficit, given the nature of the Reagan program, was to achieve the maximum in budget cuts — in other words, to undertake a wholesale attack on the welfare state. As it turned out, despite heroic efforts on Stockman's part and a good deal of success in cutting spending on education, the poor, the environment, alternative energy systems and the cities, the cuts were not drastic enough.[4] The American government deficit, as the world well knows, grew enormously.

The Costs of Reaganomics

Having looked at what the theorists had hoped for, let us examine what actually became of the Reagan revolution.

As a result of the Reagan tax cut — the Economic Recovery Tax Act of 1981 (ERTA) — the effective household tax rate fell by about 1.5 per cent. In addition, corporate taxes were sharply cut, declining by about a third as a ratio of federal government income. Between 1980 and 1984, the receipts of the U.S. federal government fell by 1.5 per cent of GNP, and despite the budget cutting efforts of the Reagan administration, the share of GNP spent by the federal government increased by 1 per cent between 1980 and 1984.[5]

The Reagan program of 1981 had been premised on a balanced budget by Fiscal Year 1984. Instead, by 1984 the federal government deficit swelled to $175 billion (5 per cent of GNP). Part of the reason for the mushrooming of the deficit was that defence spending was increased at the same time as the tax cuts were in progress. Between 1980 and 1985, defence spending grew by just over 1 per cent of GNP, increasing the American defence budget from $185 billion to $254 billion between 1982 and 1985. While the budgets for health, education, social programs and urban renewal were cut substantially, the very large rise in interest payments resulting from the rapidly rising debt of the federal government more than offset any potential saving.[6] Between 1979 and 1984, interest payments on the government deficit increased by 1.5 per cent of the GNP — from about 6 per cent of the federal budget to 10 per cent. Thus, rather than achieving balanced budgets, the Reagan revolution led the country through record deficits, mounting from $64.3 billion in 1981 to $175.8 billion in 1985.[7]

The Reagan revolution — the tax cut and the increased defence budget — were initiated at a time when the Federal Reserve Board was sharply cutting back the U.S. money supply. The Board's strategy was designed by Chairman Paul C. Volcker as a way of cutting inflation, and its action fitted perfectly with the prescriptions of orthodox monetarism. The results brought the monetarist and supply-side programs into a critical juxtaposition. The cut in the money supply succeeded in dramatically slowing economic growth, thereby launching "Volcker's recession," the downturn of 1981-82, the most severe since the Great Depression. At the same time, however, the deep recession succeeded in squeezing inflation out of the economy to an extent that would have been barely conceivable at the outset.

Simply lowering inflation by cutting the growth in the money supply would not have led to the recovery which followed the severe recession. Recovery was promoted by the supply- siders' tax cut, strongly aided by increased defence spending and declining international petroleum prices. "Reaganomics" involved both monetarist and supply- side aspects and, in fact, was an unintentional union of the two. The Reagan recovery was promoted by a huge government deficit, a fact that was to have fateful consequences for the future.

High real interest rates, promoted by tight money, acted as a magnet to draw foreign capital into the United States. As the American economy began to expand once more because of the fiscal stimulus of the Reagan program and the added bonus of the world oil price decline at the beginning of 1983, the U.S. budget deficit rapidly appreciated. In addition, the capital flow to the United States from other countries pushed up the value of the American dollar against other currencies, making conditions much more difficult for American exporters. Meanwhile, renewed U.S. economic expansion promoted an enormous increase in foreign products imported by Americans. Under the circumstances the result was a sharp rise in the merchandise trade deficit of the United States.

The rise of the budgetary and trade deficits and the impending return of the United States to net debtor status were matters of concern to experts, but did little to disturb the general euphoria. In 1983 and 1984, the great years of the Reagan recovery, the U.S. GNP grew by

3.7 per cent and then by 6.8 per cent.[8] Unemployment fell from 9.5 percent in 1983 to 7.4 per cent in 1984.[9] With renewed economic growth, most Americans seemed to forget just how severe the recession had been — a decline in real GNP of 2.1 per cent in 1982 and a simultaneous plunge in industrial production of 8.1 per cent.[10] Recovery from the recession brought lower unemployment, but even with recovery the jobless rate did not fall as low as the highest unemployment suffered during the much-despised years of the Carter presidency.

The fact was, however, that the Reagan recovery did involve the large-scale creation of new jobs, something which the recovery in Western Europe had not accomplished. In the first ten quarters (two-and-a-half years) of the recovery, beginning in the fourth quarter of 1982, civilian employment in the United States grew by 7.6 million jobs (7.7 per cent).[11] But if there was job creation in the United States, there were also very disturbing trends in employment and earnings for ordinary Americans. Nearly 60 per cent of the new jobs created between 1979 and 1984 paid less than $7,000 a year (in 1984 dollars), according to a study commissioned by the U.S. Congressional Joint Economic Committee.[12] In the period between 1973 and 1979, on the other hand, fewer than one-fifth of the new jobs paid this little.[13] Moreover, the study also showed that in the early 1980s new jobs for white men, traditionally the best paid workers in the United States, were overwhelmingly of the low paying variety — 97 per cent of them paying under $7,000 a year. Wages among both black men and women also declined, wiping out earlier gains made by blacks in winning high-wage jobs.[14]

The new jobs being created tended to be part-time work with low wages and few benefits. The Congressional study, cited above, concluded that nearly 29 per cent of all blue collar workers lost 25 per cent or more of their weekly full-time earnings during the early 1980s, and about 10 per cent lost half or more of their pay. White collar workers were hit slightly less hard with 24.4 per cent of them losing 25 per cent or more of their income and 7.4 per cent losing half or more.[15]

The harsh fact has been downward mobility for a very large proportion of Americans. The average weekly earnings of Americans have declined by 14.3 per cent since 1973, once inflation is factored out. Median household income in the United States was $26,433 in 1984, a decline in real terms of about 6 per cent since 1973. Real manufacturing wages declined by 5 per cent between 1978 and the mid-1980s, while real pay in the construction industry dropped 15 per cent.[16]

The change in the wage structure of the United States has had a marked effect on the material expectations of younger workers. Let us consider the prospects for several cohorts of thirty-year-olds as they worked their way to age forty. (All of the earning figures that follow are in 1984 dollars.) In 1949, the average thirty-year-old man earned $11,924 and reached $19,475 by age forty for an increase in earning power of 63 per cent. In 1959, the average thirty- year-old made $17,188, and $25,627 ten years later, up 49 per cent. In 1973, the average thirty-year-old earned $23,580 and ten years later was making $23,395 — a drop of 1 per cent. By 1983, the average thirty-year-old set out on an uncertain journey with an income of $17,520, almost back to the level of the thirty-year-old of 1959.[17]

But dreams die hard — the American dream the hardest of all. The striving of Americans to do well and to improve on the material well-being of their forebears remains as strong as ever. Now that American industry is faltering and incomes are falling, the road to material well-being is often via personal debt — which has been increasing rapidly in the United States. Americans have been notoriously low savers in recent years — leaving it instead to foreigners to do their saving for them. Between 1981 and 1985, American personal saving declined from 6.7 per cent to 4.8 per cent of disposable income. During the same period, the total liabilities of Americans increased from an average of 79.4 per cent to an average of 86.3 per cent of their annual incomes.[18] (Sixty per cent of the liability was accounted for by mortgages on homes with the rest based on various forms of consumer credit.) Taken together, American personal assets outweighed liabilities by a ratio of 2.24 to 1 in 1985.[19] A greater willingness to assume personal debt allowed consumer spending to increase while real incomes did not. As the British newspaper, the *Economist*, commented in early 1987, "consumers are using their credit cards to buy what their wages increasingly can't."[20] Clearly, declining savings and increasing liabilities could not be sustained indefinitely. Sooner or later, Americans were bound to wake up with a very serious economic hangover.

The American economy in the 1980s has been characterized by stagnating real incomes, low paying new jobs and mounting debt. What underlies all these problems is the decline of American industry in international terms. To understand this phenomenon, we must see it first in internal American terms and then in global terms. Inside the United

States, life has altered dramatically as people move from one set of industries to another and from declining to prospering regions of the country. In global terms, American manufacturing has been declining vis-à-vis manufacturing in Japan, western Europe and the newly industrializing countries.

Let us focus first on the shift in occupations. While, in the past an American worker might have been employed by U.S. Steel, now he or she was more likely to work for McDonald's. From 1973 to 1984, the following sectors saw the fastest increases in employment: health services; restaurants and bars; business services; state and local government; wholesale trade; food stores; hotels and lodging; and banking. In these sectors nearly 10.5 million new jobs were created, 8.5 million of them in categories which paid less than the average American wage.[21] During the same period, the big job losers were: primary metals; textile mills; clothing; railroads; fabricated metals; retailing of general merchandise; construction materials; and leather goods. In these sectors nearly 1.7 million jobs were lost, six hundred thousand of them in the high paying steel and fabricated metals sectors.[22]

The American labour force was involved in a basic shift from manufacturing to the service sector. Between 1970 and 1984, the number of Americans employed in manufacturing increased a tiny amount from 19.4 million to 19.8 million.[23] As a proportion of the non-agricultural payroll, this involved a drop from 27.4 per cent to 20.7 per cent. During the same years, employment in the service sector expanded from 41.8 million to 65.2 million jobs — from 59 per cent of the non-agricultural payroll to 68.1 per cent of it.[24]

The jobs shift was paralleled by one of the great regional migrations in American history. Millions of Americans were moving from the midwest and mid-Atlantic states — the heartland of the old smoke-stack industries — to the south and southwest, and during the latter part of the period to New England.

In the thirteen states which border on Canada, the period from 1980 to 1985 was one of blight and stagnation. While the population of the country as a whole grew by 4 per cent, the northern tier of states suffered a dismal 1.05 per cent growth rate. Where were Americans headed? Three states were the main beneficiaries — Florida, California and Texas (before the oil price plunge in early 1986 put Texas into an economic deep freeze) — absorbing 5.5 million people, or half the total population increase of the country.[25] Another region that was enjoying prosperity was New England, whose high-tech industries, particularly in the greater Boston area, took off between the mid-1970s and the mid-1980s. In New England the unemployment rate dropped from 10.2 per cent to 4.9 per cent between 1975 and 1984.[26]

How can these occupational and regional shifts be explained? One view has it that they are the by-products of a technological revolution that is renewing the American economy, making it far richer than in the past. Americans, from this perspective, have always been a migratory people, leaving old industries and regions for new ones when times change. The plight of the laid-off steel workers of South Chicago may be pitiable, but the rise of Miami and Tulsa, and the renewal of Boston, more than make up for it.

The problem with this perspective on the American economy becomes apparent as soon as we move from analysing it in American national terms to understanding it in an international context. Seen from a global perspective, the United States has clearly been experiencing economic decline, a decline which can be measured in a number of different ways. The broadest indicator is the growth of the real Gross Domestic Product (GDP) of the United States compared with that in the other major industrialized countries. In the quarter-century from 1960 to 1984, American real GDP increased, on average, by 3.3 per cent a year — lower than that of Japan (6.9), Canada (4.2), France (4.0), and Italy (3.8). The only countries the U.S. outpaced were West Germany (3.1) and Britain (2.2).[27]

The poor performance of West Germany may surprise some. A different perspective is provided when we turn to a more relevant measure — growth in real GDP per capita — which takes account of the fact that the U.S. population increased between 1960 and 1984, while West Germany's stopped growing. In real per capita GDP, U.S. growth averaged 2.1 per cent per year, behind Japan (5.8), France (3.2), Italy (3.2), Canada (2.8) and West Germany (2.7) — ahead only of Britain (1.9).[28] By 1986, the Reagan recovery had completely run out of steam and the United States ended up with per capita GDP growth of only 2.2 per cent, behind Canada, France, Japan, and West Germany, but ahead of Britain and Italy.[29]

How has the United States fared in specific sectors in comparison with other countries?

Between 1960 and 1984, American growth in real-value-added in agriculture averaged 0.9 per cent per year, tied with Japan as the lowest among the seven major industrial nations and behind Britain (2.7), Canada (2.3), Italy (1.5), France (1.5), and West Germany (1.3).[30] In industry and manufacturing for the same period, U.S. average real-value-added grew by 2.8 per cent and 3.3 per cent a year respectively — behind Japan (8.5 and 9.6), France (4.4 and 4.9), Italy (4.1 and 4.8), and Canada (3.9 and 4.1), but ahead of West Germany (2.5 and 3.2) (again a function of no labour force growth) and Britain (1.5 and 1.1).[31] In the service sector, American real- value-added increased on average by 3.6 per cent a year over this period — behind Japan (6.7), Canada (4.5), France (4.1), Italy (3.9), and West Germany (3.7), while ahead only of Britain (2.3).[32]

The per capita figures further substantiate the trend. In real-value-added per person in agriculture, U.S. growth averaged 2.9 per cent per year from 1960 to 1984 — last — behind Italy (5.8), France (5.5), West Germany (5.4), Britain (5.2) and Canada (3.7).[33] In real-value- added per person employed in industry and manufacturing (for the same period), the United States again placed last with an average growth of 1.8 per cent a year and 2.5 per cent a year respectively — behind Japan (6.4 and 7.7), France (4.4 and 5.0), Italy (4.0 and 4.9), West Germany (3.2 and 3.7), Britain (3.1 and 2.9), and Canada (2.3 and 2.6).[34] America also lagged behind in growth in real-value-added per person employed in services, with an average growth of 0.9 per cent per year — behind Japan (4.2), West Germany (2.5), France (2.3), Italy (1.9), Britain (1.1) and Canada (1.0).[35] Finally, in the aggregate category of real GDP per person employed, U.S. growth was yet again the smallest for the period examined, at an average rate of 1.3 per cent per year, below that of Japan (5.8), Italy (3.7), France (3.6), West Germany (3.3), Britain (2.2), and Canada (1.7).[36]

In the statistics presented here, the United States ranked below average growth among the major seven countries in every single category and at, or near, the bottom in most. The conclusion can only be that over the quarter-century from 1960 to 1984, the United States fell behind its major competitors in rate of growth in every single significant category of economic life. In 1960, the United States enjoyed vast economic supremacy. In the quarter-century that followed, its lead was lost or was slipping away in the major sectors of the economy.

These slower growth rates have been an important underlying cause of the deteriorating position of the United States in world trade, and in America's return to the status of a net debtor nation for the first time in over six decades. The Reagan recovery was accompanied by an unprecedented plunge in the merchandise trade balance of the United States. The Reagan revolution, it turned out, was based, not on improving American productivity, but on a spending spree in which Americans as a nation lived beyond their means. The contrast between the performance of American trade during the recovery from the 1981-2 recession and during previous recoveries was striking. In the first two years of the upturn, imports increased at the exceptionally rapid rate of 18.4 per cent a year. During earlier recoveries, they had typically increased by 6.8 per cent a year. Moreover, U.S. exports were much weaker this time around. Instead of advancing at 8.1 per cent a year, the typical rate for past upturns, they nudged ahead at an anemic 0.4 per cent a year.[37] The deterioration of the U.S. real net foreign balance amounted to 1.5 per cent of GDP per year during the first two years of the recovery.

The U.S. merchandise trade balance set off on a record breaking string of negatives: $-36.4 billion in 1982; $- 62.0 billion in 1983; $-108.3 billion in 1984; $-150 billion in 1985; and $-174 billion in 1986.[38] The implications of this mounting trade deficit are revealed when its shifting internal composition is examined. The international price of oil was falling at the same time as the American balance of trade was worsening. America's foreign oil bill fell from $61.3 billion in 1982 to $49.7 billion in 1985.[39] In 1982, the U.S. foreign oil bill exceeded the trade deficit by $25 billion. By 1985, the trade deficit was three times as great as the oil bill.

During the 1980s, American imports of manufactured products were increasing enormously, particularly imports of machinery and vehicles. In 1984, the United States imported $217.5 billion worth of manufactured goods, with imports of machinery and vehicles skyrocketing to $123.1 billion, the latter an increase of 62.6 per cent over imports in 1982.[40] The huge increase of manufactured imports resulted from two factors: the overvalued American dollar, which as we have seen was the product of the particular mix of U.S. economic policies; and the impact of the long-run deterioration of the American competitive position vis-à-vis foreign manufacturers.

Even more ominous than the merchandise trade balance was the deterioration of America's current account position and the emergence of the United States as a debtor nation. In the post World War II period, the United States has earned enormous amounts of money on its investments abroad, largely in the form of dividends and interest payments. Naturally, this has depended on the extent to which American assets abroad exceed the assets of foreigners in the United States, that is, the net international assets of the United States. In 1976, total

American assets abroad were worth $347.2 billion, while foreign assets in the United States were valued at $263.6 billion, leaving the United States with net international assets of $83.6 billion. In 1982, at the trough of the recession, American net international assets totalled $149.5 billion. From that point, as the effects of the strong dollar, high real interest rates, and the mounting trade and budget deficits did their work, the American position quickly eroded. In 1984, foreign assets in the United States were worth $904.5 billion, while American assets abroad were valued at $908.6 billion, for a net U.S. position of $4 billion. In 1985, the United States went into net debt to the tune of $124 billion and in 1986 the international debt skyrocketed to $270 billion — making the United States easily the country in the world with the largest net debt.[41]

As a country with a massive net debt, of course, the United States would soon face a deficit on the services (dividends, interest payments, travel) side of the current account as well as on the merchandise side. While in 1981, the United States had a surplus of $34 billion on the services side of the ledger, by 1986 the surplus had fallen to $6 billion. In the next few years, America's services account can be expected to add to the merchandise trade deficit rather than moderating it, as it has done up to now.

Given the rate at which the American current account deficit has been accumulating, it is not at all unreasonable to forecast a net debt for the United States of a trillion dollars, or close to it, in the next few years. Once in place, such a debt will be very difficult to overcome. Servicing the debt alone, depending on interest rates, will cost somewhere between fifty and one hundred billion dollars a year. Reducing the debt will cost much more, of course. In such a situation the United States would have to face the prospect of needing a very considerable merchandise trade surplus to keep the current account in balance. What this points to is the likelihood that Americans may soon face a very real contraction of their standard of living in order to pay for the free spending style of the Reagan recovery.

Instead of facing up to these imperatives, the Reagan administration has made matters worse by continuing to push for higher defence budgets while refusing to raise taxes. Underlying these policies has been the hope that a renewed entrepreneurial energy, resulting from lower taxes and deregulation, will save the day, making the United States the most productive of nations once again. This hope is the deepest recess of Reaganism. It is the source of continued optimism in the face of all manner of obstacles.

At bottom, deregulation adds up to an across the board quest for lower costs of production, achieved not through the development of new techniques or technology, but by removing those rules put into place to protect the environment, ensure service and safety for the public and guarantee on-the-job safety and minimum wage protection for employees. Deregulation has been closely linked with the parallel drive for de-unionization and lower labour costs.

The Reagan administration placed high hopes on deregulation from the very beginning. Major efforts were undertaken to deregulate the transportation and communication sectors in particular. But despite this policy, the American productivity performance has remained dismal during the 1980s, suggesting that the medicine the economy is receiving is not doing the job.

While it is still too early to tell if experiments in deregulation will be successful in boosting productivity in specific sectors, it is possible to conclude that one of the victims of Reaganomics has been the American trade union movement. Long before Ronald Reagan became president, American unions were in decline. In 1966, 25 per cent of American workers were unionized; by 1982, the unionized proportion of the work force was down to 16 per cent,[42] making the United States far less unionized than any other major industrial country. By the mid-1980s, only 8 per cent of the U.S. civilian labour force, or about nine million workers, were covered by major collective bargaining agreements. Moreover, the effectiveness of American unions has been sharply diminishing. Between 1979 and 1982, over one quarter of unionized workers were involved in wage and benefit concessions of various kinds.[43] Workers were faced with deferrals of wage increases, wage freezes or cuts, and with the freezing or discontinuing of cost of living (COLA) increases.

If deregulation is linked with de-unionization, the two are important causes of what economists call "real wage flexibility," a phrase which refers to the willingness of labour to make significant wage concessions. During the Reagan recovery, hourly compensation in manufacturing increased by an average of only 3.7 per cent per year, compared with the 7.6 per cent average in the three previous upturns.[44] Seen in the context of the international performance of the U.S. economy, low wage increases have been the accompaniment of poor productivity increases. It is not unfair to conclude that, for ordinary

Americans, holding down wages has been the essence of Reaganomics.

What conclusions can we draw concerning the consequences of the Reagan revolution for the United States?

During the 1980s, the Reagan administration has made a half-hearted, often inconsistent attempt to reassert what it has understood as the essential principles of the American economy. The half-heartedness stemmed from the fact that the Reagan team has always been more at home asserting American power against a host of sinister foes — the Libyans, the Sandinistas, the Angolans and sometimes the Soviet Union — than against America's capitalist competitors. Rearming has been closer to the heart of the administration than American economic competitiveness. That said, however, it should not be forgotten that second only to the arms build-up has been Ronald Reagan's adherence to tax cuts.

The combination of increased defence spending and tax cuts has been fateful. The United States, arguably, had the power to choose either to rearm, thereby asserting its power against the Soviet Union, or to pursue a carefully conceived conservative economic strategy along the lines of that followed in Margaret Thatcher's Britain, thereby asserting its power against Japan and West Germany. Under Ronald Reagan it has tried to do both, not being willing to recognize any limits on American power. The result has been that the United States, which faced severe foreign competition at the beginning of the Reagan era, is much further behind as it draws to a close. It faces a mountain of international debt — the true monument to a political movement whose very essence is an extravagant assessment of the American place in the world.

Still, while the Reagan administration has done much to undermine the position of the American economy in the world, it did not create the basic problems that America faces. To understand what America is up against in the late 20th century, we need to come to grips with the American economic mentality, with the American idea of the economy. That is the subject of the next chapter.

Chapter Two

Flight of the Eagle: The American Idea of the Economy

The passing of an age is difficult to understand because it destroys the assumptions we make about the world. To deal with such an event, we need new bearings, a new compass to interpret what we see around us.

On July 4, 1986 U.S. President Ronald Reagan presided at gargantuan patriotic celebrations in New York City whose highlight was one of the greatest fireworks displays in history over the re-dedicated Statue of Liberty. The theme of the celebrations, like the theme of the Reagan administration, was that America now stood "tall in the saddle again." Few of those watching would have agreed with the assertion that the United States had entered an era of historical decline. Yet the Americans who watched the fireworks on that warm July evening were much like the British who gloried in the grandiose celebrations of Queen Victoria's Diamond Jubilee in London in 1897. Despite the pomp on that greatest of imperial occasions, Britain by the end of the 19th century was on a downward slide. In both cases — London in 1897 and New York in 1986 — much though the celebrants would have denied it, the mammoth displays glorified a global domination which had passed its peak and was already receding.

Discussing America's decline before analysing its rise puts the cart before the horse. What was it that made America uniquely successful in the two centuries following the American revolution, taking the United States from a colonial nation of three million people to a world superpower of 240 million? The opening up of a land of immense

resources was, of course, a large part of the story. But no less important was the mentality and the social organization of Americans. What
concerns us here is the development of the critical assumptions about
economy and society that today are virtually second nature in America.

The Historical Record

The founding of America involved a mixture of motives, both
materialistic and philosophical, which can be seen in the histories of
the colonies before the American revolution. While one can readily see
the profit motive at work in early Virginia, both on the part of the set-
tlers and those in England who financed them, the Puritan settlements
in New England were in large measure driven by the quest for freedom
from persecution. Looked at in isolation, the thirteen colonies out of
which the new nation was established exhibited wide diversity. Yet,
seen from the wider perspective of their European background, their
singular focus becomes much more apparent. Here were societies that
were capitalist from the start, in a focused way that was different from
the hybrid social character of the Europe they had left behind. The
colonies were entirely post-feudal. No genuine aristocracy ever existed
among them. Virginia's wealthy tobacco planters were closer than
anyone else in colonial America to an aristocracy. But even they owed
their position to business prowess rather than hereditary position.[1] In
America there was, from the start, private ownership of land, manufacturing establishments and commercial ventures. It was a society rooted
in individualism, in the notion that the good and the just would
demonstrate their worthiness through diligence and hard work. There
was little sympathy for sinners and for those who did not demonstrate
a capacity for self-help. There was also — and this was at the root of
the American mentality as it developed in colonial times — a practi-
cal insistence on trying what worked and not assuming too much of
the basis on theory. This pragmatism, the inheritance of English Protes-
tantism, was applied in the environment of a new world — where nature, climate and geography demanded constant adaptation and the
rejection of old forms of thought. Here was a new society that would
not accept elitism in thought any more than it could accept aristocratic
forms of social organization.

What was being established were the habits of thought, the attitudes which would distinguish America from Europe and would give
the new country the sense that it was a special place, an alternative to
the corruption of the old world. Later, the struggle for independence

was to amplify these notions, to transform them into a national ideology in which the United States alternately perceived itself as a haven from the rest of the world or as a force which would liberate humanity.

The most distinguishing feature of the American character was not the Declaration of Independence or the constitution, but an institution that could easily be overlooked — the marketplace. The market economy is so central to America that it can be regarded simply as a given, almost as a part of nature. And yet it was the centrality of the marketplace to America that tied together the system of private ownership, the Protestant sensibility and the concept of limited government. In the final analysis, throwing off the fetters of Europe meant removing the remaining limitations on the freedom of the marketplace. What emerged in America during and following the era of the revolution was a dual conception of human equality. On the one hand, equality meant freedom to compete without restriction in the marketplace; and, on the other hand, equality had a wider meaning having to do with the essential worth of each person. Throughout American history both of these concepts have been in evidence. In our own era it is easy to see that the marketplace notion of equality has been gaining in ascendancy. Neo- conservatism is precisely rooted in the idea that, in preference to following a political route to achieve greater equality, Americans should unleash the power of the market to better their situation. Alone of the great nations of the world, the United States has been an entirely capitalist society. In a basic sense, American society has been the market writ large. The market does not have to justify itself in the same way as elsewhere because American society is the market.

The ending of the colonial period allowed America to proceed during the 19th century with a nation-building program that featured the conquest of the continent. Naturally, the settling of the continent was of great importance because it made the United States the master of a uniquely advantageous material environment. By the late 19th century the United States had carved out the world's largest national market, a market well suited to the rapid development of corporate capitalism. By that date, U.S. production of coal, steel and other industrial goods far outstripped that in the great powers of Europe.

The settlement of the continent also became the central experience from which sprang a strengthened national identity. The settling of the west was both an affirmation of America and a rejection of the European past. The frontier was celebrated as the place where America was continually re-created, with all its essential elements intact — individuals coming together to make a compact for a limited government, which could protect them while they pursued their own ambitions. In the work of American historian Frederick Jackson Turner, the American frontier was seen as the element in American society which most radically separated it from Europe. According to this view, the frontier transformed the whole of the country, making it thereby more American and less European. In Turnerian terms, historian Daniel J. Boorstin has drawn the lesson: "By the early 19th century, in crowded, pre- empted Europe, 'No Trespassing' signs were everywhere; control by government covered the map. America offered a sharp contrast. From the beginning, communities existed here before there were governments to care for public needs or to enforce public duties. This order of events was hardly possible in modern Europe; in America, it was normal."[2]

Just what were the values of this American frontier, as presented by historians and myth-makers? Even though groups and communities were key to settlement, the cultural hero who survives in the American imagination has been the self-reliant individual operating in a setting where eastern breeding or European manners and culture counted for little. Here was a new country of heroic proportions in which small towns could grow in a few decades into giants such as Chicago, Denver or Minneapolis. For the booster entrepreneurs who promoted such towns, there was no sharp line between private and community interest. A uniquely American type of businessman, the central mover and shaker of the society, profited from real estate booms, railway schemes and industrial development. What would later be called the "private sector" lived its great days with impresario entrepreneurs such as William B. Ogden, the promoter of mid-19th-century Chicago, at the centre.[3]

The American idea of progress and democracy was shaped around these archetypal figures. What was emerging was a notion of freedom of enterprise that was double-edged — expressing a democratic rejection of societies where family ties or social background determined one's fate, along with disdain for those who sought to form combinations to serve collective interests. This heady brew of fact and myth turned on assumed polarities — the individual versus the mass and business versus government. Government and the mass were forces for inertia, or, even worse, barriers to freedom, while business and the individual were symbols of progress and material well-being. Here were the values out of which recurrent waves of American conservatism would draw their inspiration. When technology and industrial organization had created a world that would have been unrecognizable to the mid-19th century boosters, the simple lessons of the period would remain a potent force in history.

If the myth of the frontier was to play a major role in the cultural differentiation of America from Europe, the struggle against the South and slavery was to further refine America as a society of unfettered capitalism. Northern outrage depicted slavery as an evil violation of the rights of human beings, an affront to the idea that all people are equal in the eyes of God. Slavery was also denounced as a barrier to the operations of the marketplace, a roadblock in the path of free labour, a force which stifled enterprise. The Civil War removed the divisiveness at the heart of American life that had been the consequence of the South's " peculiar institution." Victory for the North meant victory for the marketplace society throughout the United States.

The war was followed by the rise of large scale American business. In the age of the so-called "robber barons" — the Rockefellers and Carnegies — the new industrial techniques of the late 19th century were harnessed by trusts in the railroads, and the oil, steel, tobacco, meat packing and chemical industries. The hallmarks of this classical age of American industrialism were the lavish use of raw materials, the refining of the techniques of factory production, deployment of unskilled labour on a huge scale, the production of uniform, low-cost commodities.

The techniques employed in American industry were to make it unique. The development of what came to be the American factory system, called the "American system" by Europeans, stemmed initially from American backwardness. The United States lacked skilled artisans in anything like the numbers of England. Furthermore, the new nation did not have a plentiful supply of cheap labour. Labour did not come at a low price because, until well into the 19th century, labourers had the option of virtually free land and migration to the west.

But the combination of high cost labour with few skilled artisans proved to be a barrier that sparked innovation and breakthrough. In the late 18th century, Eli Whitney, inventor and mass producer of the cotton gin, was the key figure in the formulation of the new system.

Historian Daniel J. Boorstin has elaborated the principles of the new American way: "Where labour was scarce, where a man was expected to turn easily from one task to another, his machines had to possess the competence he lacked. Whitney's Interchangeable System, as he himself explained, was 'a plan which is unknown in Europe and the great leading object of which is to substitute correct and effective operations of machinery for that skill of the artist which is acquired only by long practice and experience, a species of skill which is not possessed in this country to any considerable extent.' "[4]

As Boorstin concluded, the new system went a long way to wiping out the distinction between skilled and unskilled labour, making the old crafts obsolete. The American factory system was to change the world.

In his book *The Next American Frontier*, Robert Reich identifies three key factors underlying the historical success of American business: specialization by simplification; predetermined rules; and management information.[5]

Specialization by simplification refers to the breaking down of the steps involved in production into finite simple units. By identifying the mechanical movements required for production, enterprises were able to employ inexperienced and unskilled workers. Simplification of tasks made possible the efficient meshing of stages of production and use of machines by workers. It also made possible direct and effective supervision from above.

Predetermined rules allowed the simplified process of production to be monitored and controlled through a pyramidal management structure. The jobs of each level in the structure were carefully defined and tasks simplified so that top management knew exactly what was being done on each rung of the productive ladder.

Management information was the means by which those at the top collected the data necessary to apply the rules for the division of tasks, so that the simple steps of production could be most efficiently undertaken. Systems for collecting information were crucial to the functioning of the whole.

American enterprise relied on dependable repetition. Its hierarchical structure and flow of orders allowed for precious little creative input from below. In fact, creative input from below was not valued. The approach achieved its highest theoretical summation in the notions of Frederick Taylor. Taylor carried out time-motion studies to work out the exact number of movements a worker needed to carry out a particular task. Whether it was working with a shovel, or doing some other mechanical job, the idea was to eliminate any independent approach on the part of the workers, so that the job could be done dependably, efficiently and in uniform bits of time. In his book *The Principles of*

Scientific Management, published in 1911, Taylor proclaimed that "in the past the man has been first; in the future the system must be first."[6] With the innovations of Henry Ford in designing the flowing production of the assembly line, the timing of each task was crucial, because it determined the speed at which the line could run.

American industrial technique became supreme in the world during the period from the end of the Civil War to the outbreak of the Great Depression in 1929. Not only was the American market uniquely large, the growth rates achieved by the U.S. economy as a whole were regularly higher than those in other industrial nations. For example, from 1900 to 1913, total output in the United States grew at an average of 3.98 per cent a year, compared with Germany (2.91), France (2.63), Italy (2.59) and Britain (1.53).[7] Again in the 1920s, the United States achieved an average rate of growth of 3.76 per cent, below France (5.91), and Germany (4.08), but ahead of Italy (2.59) and Britain (1.74).[8]

Of course, American development involved much more than the harnessing of new industrial techniques to serve a giant market. During the 20th century, the United States was to project its power, its conception of society onto the rest of the world, with enormous consequences. Our discussion is incomplete, therefore, without a brief consideration of the rise of America to the status of a superpower.

American history in this century has turned on a great irony: the nation that was forged in the first anti- imperial revolution of modern times was itself to achieve a greater sway over other nations than any country ever had. In the past, this would have been described as an "empire." But, to American ears, the word "empire" is pejorative. It smacks of kings, aristocrats and armies conquering wretched natives. To accuse a nation of free people of establishing an empire can only be a slur, a contradiction in terms. Nonetheless, despite this overt American hostility to empire, an attitude which has survived until the late 20th century, the United States began, quite early in its history, to establish its power over other countries. This process occurred in a number of stages:

- First came the territorial expansion of the United States itself. American expansion in the 19th century was punctuated by wars against the Indians, purchases of territory from European powers, and wars against Britain, Mexico and Spain.

- Next came the notion that the United States had a special role to play in defending the western hemisphere from interference by outside powers. This idea was already developing while Americans pushed west across the continent. Its classical expression came in 1823 in the Monroe Doctrine, which stated that the United States would not tolerate interference in the affairs of the western hemisphere by any European power not already established there. In its first enunciation, the Monroe Doctrine had a defensive connotation. It was a warning to Spain to leave its former Latin American colonies alone. Later, however, the doctrine was to serve as a cover for numerous American military incursions into Latin American countries. Often American intervention was presented as a necessary response to the threat of outside interference (most recently against Soviet interference in central America), but the underlying idea was clear: the United States felt that it had the right to impose sympathetic regimes on Latin America. Such American intervention did not involve classical imperialism — there was no annexing of territory, no creation of formal colonies, over which the Stars and Stripes flew. Yet, there was a clear designation of the Western Hemisphere as a special American preserve, a region of the world in which outside powers must tread warily.

- During the third stage, America projected its power outside the western hemisphere. This began in a major way in World War I, which the United States entered in 1917, an intervention that was decisive in achieving the defeat of the German Empire and its allies. After the peace settlement of 1919, the Americans withdrew into their customary isolation from European affairs, not even joining the League of Nations (the brainchild of American President Woodrow Wilson). Permanent American intervention worldwide came only with U.S. participation in the Second World War and its aftermath.

In 1945 the United States achieved dominance on a global scale — greater than any power in history. At the end of the war, Japan and Germany lay in ruins and the British empire was tottering, with Britain itself exhausted and in debt. Only the Soviet Union, a country with a backward economy, was in any position to stay outside the sphere of American power, and to define its own, although lesser sphere.

In the mid-20th century American international sphere, the notion of the marketplace society was to be elevated to a central position. As already indicated, the American- designed international economic system was premised on the twin notions of free movement of capital and free trade. And these pillars were nothing more than the means by which the world could be made safe for the marketplace. As we will see in later chapters, a high priority in American post-war economic policy was to redesign the corporate structures of West Germany and Japan, so that they conformed to the American practice.

If the market gave the American sphere cohesion within, rivalry with the Soviet Union encouraged unity against external opposition. The Soviet Union's rejection of the marketplace made it a perfect symbol of unfreedom. For the United States, the Soviet Union and the threat it posed reinforced the moral purpose behind the exercise of American power in the world. Indeed that moral purpose had been reinforced by recent history, by the failure of the other capitalist states to achieve a peaceful order among themselves in the inter-war years. This failure had put the old fashioned nation states into disgrace and it opened the way for the hegemony of the United States.

Origins of American Decline

Ironically, the very ideas which were at the centre of the American global system help to explain the decline of American economic power in the decades since the war. As a result of their history, Americans have elevated crucial ideas about the operation of their economy to the level of axioms — that is, they have placed them on a pedestal where they are beyond debate. In such a fashion, Americans have held these truths to be self-evident:

- that the private sector is necessarily superior to the public sector in carrying out productive economic tasks.

- that government intervention in the economy, to target particular long-term goals or to overcome backwardness in specific sectors, cannot be superior to the simple workings of the market system.

- that private-public planning to set priorities for the long-range development of the economy cannot pick "winners" as well as the market can.

- An agency of the state, or a cooperatively owned enterprise, cannot be as efficient as one operating in the private sector. Publicly owned companies are not motivated by the need to produce a profit because they can always turn to government for handouts. They are confused by contradictory goals: the drive for efficiency versus the need to serve public policy ends. The managers of public companies are bureaucrats who cannot understand production the way private sector managers can.

As a consequence of these axiomatic beliefs, the United States has rejected the notion of an "industrial strategy," of an approach which combines private enterprise with public sector intervention. What makes this an important matter is that, since the Second World War, all of the other advanced industrial countries, with the exception of Britain, have pursued such economic strategies. Furthermore, since the early post-war years, all of these countries, including Japan and the major nations of western Europe, have achieved higher rates of economic development and productivity growth than the United States.

To explain American decline, we offer the following two- pronged hypothesis:

- American history and experience has created a frame of mind which makes it extremely difficult for Americans to have an empathic understanding of other societies and their forms of social organization.

- The American belief in the market system has become a faith whose beneficial character has become axiomatic and is therefore not tested against the performance of other societies. The power of the United States has ebbed because Americans have relied too much on the marketplace alone to set the goals for their society. Suffering from a national myopia, the United States has been consumed with the pursuit of its advantage in the short term, while the long term has been allowed to take care of itself. The result is a loss of direction in American society, a loss of direction which by the late 20th century has allowed other industrialized countries to take the lead in key aspects of economic life.

The story of the decades since the Second World War is that of the development of coherent economic strategies in Western Europe and East Asia which have proven themselves at least a match for that of the United States — and, characteristically, of American bewilderment in the face of successful foreign competition.

In the subsequent undoing of American economic supremacy, the following sets of factors proved to be of decisive importance:

- The investment decisions and management techniques of American business compared with business in other countries.

- The absence of an industrial strategy in the United States like that pursued in other countries.

- The immense American military budget compared with that of other leading capitalist countries.

Let us look further at each of these factors, beginning with the record of American corporate management.

The United States entered the post-war period with enormous advantages. This was the golden era of U.S. multi-national corporations, an era when the global economy was dominated by American management techniques, American managers and American technology. Yet the supremacy of American business bred problems. At the pinnacle of global business, American management tended to assume that nothing could ever displace it from its lofty position. American managers began to take production in their facilities for granted, turning their attention ever more toward the financial and accounting side of their businesses. Success was coming to be measured in terms of returns to the company from quarter to quarter. Many of the most talented managers specialized in "money" rather than production, becoming wizards of mergers, takeovers and the blocking of takeovers. Furthermore, as was appropriate for a nation inspired by the individualist ethic, the emphasis among business managers was on their personal success. Their ambitions reinforced the tendency to act for the short term rather than to plan for the future. Business managers tended to move often from firm to firm. What looked good on their records, therefore, was success in improving the company's bottom line performance in the short term.

The problem was that the development of whole new lines of products, or new techniques of production, required large investments which in the short term hurt the company bottom line. Little matter that someday the company, and the country, would benefit from such investment. By the time it paid off, the manager who had made the decision could be long gone to another firm and someone else would get the credit. The tendency, then, was for American companies to have cautious investment strategies that emphasized product imitation (to go after existing markets) rather than bold attempts at innovation (to create markets for new products).

There was another reason for the growing concern with the short-term bottom line. Increasingly, top American managers were accountant and business school graduates rather than engineers with hands-on production experience. Consequently, decisions surrounding productive investments tended to be reduced to abstractions, based on the application of fashionable discounting techniques. Managers now made decisions by discounting estimated cash flows for a specific proposed investment. Once taxes and depreciation were subtracted from expected cash flow, the rate of return for the investment was calculated. If the expected rate of return was too low, the project was rejected. Such discounting techniques, now virtually universal in American business, tend to point companies in the direction of safe, short-term or imitative investment and away from long-term, innovative and risky investment. This "accountant" mentality has given undue emphasis to the quantitative over the qualitative. It works fine until someone else comes up with a major technological or product innovation — and then it leaves you dead in the water. In a celebrated article in the *Harvard Business Review* in the early 1980s, C.J. Grayson, president of the American Productivity Center, was quoted as saying that American management has "coasted off the great R and D gains made during World War II, and constantly rewarded executives from the marketing, financial, and legal sides of the business while it ignored the production men."[9]

The performance and mentality of American managers was only one reason for the decline of the American economy. Of great importance as well was the absence in the United States of a positive industrial strategy of the kind being pursued in other successful industrial economies.

In the United States the very concept of an industrial strategy is anathema. According to American ideology, the market system is the most perfect way to pick winners and losers and to allocate resources. An industrial strategy, on the other hand, by definition, involves interference with the market. It makes sense only if the market, by itself, is seen as insufficient to guarantee maximum long- term economic efficiency.

Japan and the major western European countries (except Britain) have pursued industrial strategies more completely and explicitly at some times than at others. Nonetheless, over the years they have demonstrated less faith in the market than the United States has. The key components of their industrial strategies are as follows:

- variable tax rates for different types of businesses to encourage investment in particular industries where long-term growth is sought.

- government procurement programs in which domestic firms receive favoured treatment in the awarding of public-sector contracts.

- favourable loans sometimes involving state agencies and sometimes private banks. The purpose of the loans is to provide capital for long-term industrial development.

- coordination by the state of forums involving business, labour and government whose purpose is to identify favourable global market opportunities. Once a potential market "niche" has been picked, a whole host of measures can be deployed to realize it.

- joint ventures involving the private and public sectors to give additional backing to projects that need them. In some cases, outright public ownership is used.

Some countries have pursued industrial strategies which are highly explicit, involving a direct effort on behalf of the government and the private sector to achieve success in a particular field. In other countries, industrial strategies have been indirect, aimed at fostering business-labour cooperation, backed up by government assistance to help promote industrial innovation. Whether of the direct or indirect variety, however, such industrial strategies act on the assumption that the market alone will not assure critical elements of economic development. Specific examples of successful industrial strategies include: the development of industrial robots in Japan; the Western European challenge to American supremacy in the building of commercial aircraft; the development of the world's fastest trains in France; and the restructuring of the Swedish economy away from industries such as steel in favour of high technology sectors, without the creation of high unemployment.

A final word must be said on the subject of the United States and industrial strategy. There has been one enormously important exception to U.S. commitment to the free-market system. That exception, of course, is defence spending, which constitutes a virtual second national American economy, of immense size. In 1985, the United States spent $284.7 billion on defence, which amounted to 6.6 per cent of the GNP and 26.5 per cent of federal government spending.[10] Military spending on this scale has provided a backdoor route by which immense sums of public-sector money can be pumped into industry and industrial research and development. Such spending has been associated with so-called "spinoffs" for the non-military sectors of the economy.

But how great are the benefits? How efficient is the "spinoff" route to industrial breakthroughs, in comparison to the direct route taken by America's leading competitors? This question did not appear to matter much in the days of massive American industrial superiority. However, now that the other advanced industrial countries have essentially caught up with the United States, the question is crucial. Research and development — the technological heart of the military budget — accounted for $24.6 billion in 1985, 8.6 per cent of all defence spending.[11] In a world in which the United States is struggling to regain its international competitiveness, this route to research and development (R and D) funding presents apparent difficulties. First, the proportion of defence spending directed to R and D is low. Second, military R and D spending is directed not at developing technology and products for use in the civilian economy, but for the development of weapons systems, many of them now highly arcane. Only a relatively small proportion of this R and D effort ends up being useful for non-military economic efforts — the "spinoff" route to new technology and product lines is extremely inefficient.

In the mid-1980s, both the United States and Japan were spending about 2.6 per cent of their respective GNP on research and development.[12] However, one-third of all American R and D is military,[13] whereas Japan spends only 1 per cent of its GNP on defence — less than one-sixth the scale of the American effort. What this means is that, the highly competitive Japanese have taken the direct route to technology and product development for a very large proportion of their R and D effort, while the Americans are relying on the indirect, inefficient spinoff route.

Defence spending is so extensive in the United States that kicking the habit would be very difficult from an economic standpoint. Whole regions of the country and entire industries have become enormously dependent on defence outlays. Defence spending has become a key method by which Presidents reward their home states. These phenonema are illustrated by following statistics for 1983:

- Just under one million workers were employed in defence industries.

- Shipments to the defence department from contracting firms were valued at $87.5 billion (about the same as the GNP of South Korea).

- The American aerospace industry was hugely dependent on defence outlays with $28.3 billion worth of the industry's products going to the defence effort.

- President Ronald Reagan's home state of California was the source of $23.9 billion worth of industrial products for the defence department. Production in California's defence sector jumped by over $10 billion during Reagan's first two years in office.[14]

Military contracts have tended to encourage wastefulness in the American economy. Contracts for the development of new weapons systems have been notoriously prone to vast cost overruns. In effect, American military contractors have operated on a cost-plus basis, earning large profits with little incentive to keep costs down. Such a system exaggerates the very worst features of public-sector spending. It has allowed waste on a scale that would not be tolerated in the industrial strategies of other nations.

Given American ideological opposition to the straightforward pursuit of an industrial strategy, it is understandable that military spending has served as a substitute. The defence of the American way of life has been an ideologically permissible use of state power. Therefore, the expenditure of huge sums for military hardware and related research and development has been politically attractive, especially to the conservative segments of the American population which are most critical of other forms of state economic intervention.

Taken together, the behaviour of American management, the absence of an industrial strategy, and the drain of military spending have brought about a long-term and qualitative weakening of the American economy compared with its leading competitors. The United States entered the post-war period prepared to defend itself and its allies and dependents against the rival system of the Soviet Union. What Americans were not prepared for was the prospect of having to defend themselves against the economic success of their allies, countries that in 1945 had little power at their disposal.

The United States has a highly developed proclivity for shutting out information about the outside world. Those who are at the zenith in any realm of human affairs are vulnerable to the twin ailments of the supremely successful — complacency and rigidity. In general, those who have succeeded in achieving mastery cannot imagine that they might ever lose it. Great power does not tend to breed long-term perspective, rather the opposite.

Only in the mid-1980s, with the extraordinary rise of Japan, have Americans begun to consider seriously the question of foreign competition. And characteristically, much of that consideration is resentment at the very idea that another country could successfully challenge American economic prowess. Here are a few of the most common American rationalizations for the success of foreign competitors, in particular the Japanese:

• Foreign economies are merely catching up with the use of
  American know-how.

- Cheap labour is the reason for many foreign successes. Foreigners could never compete with the United States if they had to pay as much for their labour as Americans pay.

- Foreigners frequently do well because, in effect, they cheat in trading with the United States. While foreign countries pursue a hard-nosed strategy of exporting to the United States, they keep their own markets substantially closed to American products.

Since the American market system was assumed to be the best possible, these rationalizations were natural enough. What was not considered, what could not be considered, was the possibility that other nations had devised economic strategies intrinsically superior to that of the United States.

Chapter Three

Britain: Once Number One

In the spring of 1987, Britain's economy was growing at an annual rate of 3.5 per cent. It was not a remarkably high growth rate, but what made it noteworthy was that, for the moment, it was the fastest rate of growth in any of the seven major industrialized countries. On the strength of this performance, some people were saying that Britain had ended its long economic decline, had broken the deadlock in British society between intransigent unions and insensitive management that had held it back, and that the country was now charting a new course of expansion for the future.

For professionals and service employees around the city of London, Britain's thriving financial centre, times indeed were good. They were benefitting from their association with one industry in Britain that was truly world class — financial markets and insurance. Had Britain been a small island around the city of London, it might have made sense even to speak of the British "miracle," as in the past one spoke of German, Japanese, French and Italian miracles. Britain, however, is much more than the City of London. When the economic record of the country as a whole is looked at, the picture is one of deepening gloom.

Britain's long-term economic experience is of general significance because the country was the site of the world's first industrial revolution, and because during much of the 19th century Britain played the role in the global economy that the United States has played since the Second World War. The British experience illustrates that decline from the top rung of the economic ladder is indeed possible and that it can be agonizingly protracted. Moreover, as we shall see, there were important similarities between the posture of British industry in the late

19th century and American industry in the late 20th century. Finally, Britain's recent experience is significant because the country has been the site for the Thatcher "revolution," the most consistent attempt anywhere to reverse economic decline by reverting to the principles of an enterprise economy with as little state intervention as possible.

The Dismal Road

Nowhere is England greener in summer than in the hills that overlook the Tong Valley in Lancashire. Here, the air is clear as one looks in the distance toward the grey shapes of Manchester. This pastoral setting now shows little evidence of being the birthplace, two centuries ago, of the industrial revolution. In the 19th century the Tong Valley was shrouded in smoke from the dozens of smokestacks that spewed forth from the "dark, satanic mills" where workers toiled twelve hours a day, six days a week. The cotton textiles they produced dominated the economic world. In 1830, 50 per cent of all British exports were textiles. Now the mills are silent, the world's highly automated cotton industry having long since shifted its main production areas to Asia. Almost the only place one can feel what the Lancashire of the past was like is in the odd mill restored as a museum for school children to visit.

Britain's industrial revolution was, of course, primitive by today's standards. Capital investment was not high. Production methods were elementary. And yet, what was achieved transformed the world. A global market was established, in part because of the efficiency of the mills of Lancashire, and in part because of the use of force, on occasion, to eliminate competitors. While cotton was the most important item in this first industrial revolution, there were other key industries — iron and steel, coal, railway components and shipbuilding. Britain succeeded in taking simple industrial processes and using them as a means to mass produce a few commodities which could then be sold around the globe.

The golden age of British industry was also a highpoint for British political and economic theory. Much of the economic wisdom which remains commonplace in the English-speaking world in the late 20th century was formulated in the mid- Victorian era. The so-called "little Englanders," writers such as Fox, Bright and Cobden, advocated the economics of laissez-faire and free trade. They had little use for the empire, where the flag flew largely for the benefit of the sons of the English rich who were ill occupied at home. They saw that Britain's economic strength lay in its competitive prowess, in its ability to purchase raw materials from anywhere and to sell into any market at the lowest price. Removing the legal fetters left over from the age of mercantilism in favour of the free market and free trade would liberate industry and enrich Britain. Free markets and free trade — the two key notions of neo- classical economists of our own age — would guarantee the most efficient worldwide allocation of resources and would even protect world peace. The market, then, was a thing of perfection to the Anglo-Saxon mind, an institution which combined both pragmatic and ethical soundness.

Mid-Victorian Britain's prowess was without equal, but it did not remain unchallenged for long. By 1880, what would prove to be the successful challenge to British industrial dominance was well underway. The rise of competitive manufacturing sectors, especially in Germany and the United States, coincided with important developments in technology. The key sectors for this transformation were chemicals, electrical products and, at the turn of the century, automobiles. These new industries depended on science, and research and development, to a much greater extent than the early industries had. They required greater amounts of capital investment and their methods of production were much more sophisticated. Such industries needed larger numbers of skilled technicians and skilled workers than in the past.

While Germany and the United States moved confidently into the new sectors, British industry was much more hesitant. In 1913, on the eve of World War I, Britain still relied very heavily on the old industries for its exports, with no less than 48.8 per cent being made up of textiles; the other major British exports were coal and metals.[1] Furthermore, even in the metals industry, where Britain was relatively strong, new steel-making techniques revolutionized an old industry. German and American steel-makers opened new, larger and technically more advanced, steel-making facilities, and these countries soon outpaced British steel production.

Britain's manufacturing output grew much more slowly than that of its competitors in the decades prior to World War I. In 1911, while the volume of British manufacturing was 60 per cent greater than it had been in the early 1880s, in Germany it was 360 per cent greater, and in the United States it had grown by nearly 380 per cent.[2]

Comparatively slow growth continued to trouble British industry in the years between the world wars. To be sure, there was some adjustment to the newer industrialism and there were some successes. The automobile industry doubled its workforce between 1923 and

1938, increasing its output from 150,000 vehicles in the mid-1920s to 493,000 vehicles in 1937. The chemical industry also grew and was reorganized into larger, more effective units, with the creation of Imperial Chemical Industries in 1926 and later the establishment of companies such as Courtaulds. But while these achievements were a part of the picture, the woes of traditional industries made the period one of painful transition. In Britain, the Great Depression had a devastating impact on employment in textiles and coal.

British decline was sharply accelerated by the Second World War. Even though Britain emerged as one of the victors, the British empire was no longer viable in the new era, and the country's financial resources were severely depleted, leaving Britain indebted to and dependent on the United States. Three factors were to have crucial importance in shaping Britain's fate in the post-war period: the country's weakness vis-à-vis the United States; the domestic consequences of the British class structure; and the absence of a genuine impulse towards industrial planning.

The first factor, the international position of Great Britain, was a direct legacy of the war. From the early days of the conflict, Britain had become dependent on American lend-lease. Moreover, as the war effort had dragged on, the United States had gained steadily in military and economic power vis-à-vis Britain. Even though Britain was involved in consultations about the structure of the post-war international economic system, the fact was that the country's indebtedness and desperate need for imports allowed the United States to keep it on a short leash. At the end of the war Britain was granted a much- needed loan of one billion dollars by the United States only in return for an undertaking that the country would move quickly to full convertibility of its currency. American leaders were not particularly sympathetic to Britain, and many of them wanted to see the old British Empire liquidated as quickly as possible. Forcing Britain into the new world of convertible currencies, freer trade and unrestricted foreign (American) investment was a way of guaranteeing that Britain's empire would not survive as a coherent economic entity. A system of open doors to currency conversion and to capital flows would promote the dominance of the strongest power, which in this period, without doubt, was the United States. Ironically, American leaders were much more hostile, in practice, to the economic integrity of the British Empire than they were to the economic revival of the defeated powers.

If Britain's position in the world necessitated going along with an American-designed international economy, its internal reality was the legacy of a class-divided society. Social classes in Britain had a sharply defined character that made them quite different from their counterparts in other advanced industrial nations. The British working class was noteworthy for its strong sense of identification, its cultural separateness, and often even for its hostility toward the very idea of upward mobility into other social classes. The upper class, for its part, was not purely an aggregation of the top levels of business. The older, pre-capitalist landed aristocracy had survived and had successfully absorbed generations of top businessmen into its ranks. What emerged was not quite a business class in the normal sense, and not quite an aristocracy, but an amalgam of the two. This top layer of British society was marked off from the rest of the nation in culture, education and lifestyle as well as in economic power and well-being.

It was paradoxical that the British capitalists of the 19th century, those "titans of industry" who transformed the world by presiding over the first industrial revolution, maintained very traditional aspirations for themselves. They remained caught up in what they saw as the superior ethic of the landed aristocracy, and the greatest ambition was to leave the grubby world of trade behind and assume the lifestyle of a peer. What was significant about these capitalists, as Anthony Simpson has written, "was the continuity of an aristocratic or would-be aristocratic tradition which while being enriched by trade still kept it at arm's length, and returned to country roots in search of more lasting values."[3]

The peculiar character of the British capitalist class was to have a marked, long-term impact on its relationship to labour. British management, with its aristocratic pretensions, adopted what amounted to a military tone toward workers — men of a higher class commanding others of a lower class. This sharp cultural and social division between management and labour widened the usual employer – employee gap into an unbridgeable chasm. Needless to say, this did not contribute to worker productivity, let alone to production. There developed a poisoned atmosphere of industrial relations that reinforced the tendency of British industry toward conservatism, making increased productivity much more difficult to achieve than in societies with a greater degree of cooperation between workers and employers.

The practices of British management during the era of industrialization and the resistance to those practices by the working class left an enduring legacy. The collision of capital and labour in the context of the British political system has resulted in social deadlock. British capitalism has been too strong to be overturned; and yet the British working class cannot be ignored.   Management cannot transcend its elitism and labour cannot accept a share of responsibility for the well-being of business. It is not unreasonable to regard British trade unionism as a mirror opposite to British management. According to British trade union tradition, capital and labour are completely separate, with few, if any, mutual interests. Accordingly, attempts at cooperation between the two sides are cast as "class collaboration," as ploys to co-opt the workers. Anthony Sampson has written that most British trade union leaders "have come to assume that higher productivity will mean higher unemployment, that higher profits will not mean higher wages, and that therefore their most important power is the power to prevent change."[4]

The war effort of 1939-45, carried out under a "national" government in which the Labour Party participated, guaranteed that British society could not simply continue unchanged once the conflict ended. The organized political and industrial strength of the working classes was too great for that, necessitating a shift in power. Both the mainstream of the Labour Party and the mainstream of the Conservative Party could agree on the need for the welfare state, while disagreeing, at times bitterly, on how rapidly it should be extended.

The Beveridge Report on social insurance in 1942, sponsored as a morale raiser by the National government during the darkest days of the war, advocated a society of greater compassion once victory had been achieved. Dealing with the problems it depicted dramatically as the five "giants" — "want," "sickness," "squalor," "ignorance" and "idleness" — the Report proposed a system of universal social security to cover everyone in the country. Specifically, the Report called for a national health service and for economic policies aimed at preventing mass unemployment.

If the Beveridge Report provided much of what was to be the postwar government's agenda, the stunning electoral defeat of Winston Churchill, the wartime hero, in the spring of 1945, just weeks after the fall of Berlin and before the war against Japan had ended, revealed the depth of the popular demand for change. Under the leadership of Clement Attlee, the first majority Labour government in the country's history came to power on a program of widespread nationalization of major industries. Once in power, however, the Labour Party's performance turned out to be much less threatening to the established order than its rhetoric had suggested. Instead of nationalizing the growth sectors of the British economy, as the program of the party had called for, the Attlee government used public ownership, for the most part, as a tool for bailing out failing industries. In 1946, in this spirit, the government nationalized the long ailing coal industry.

In the end the Labour government did not pursue a new economic strategy. It invested money all over the country in industries that usually represented the past, binding up the all too numerous sores that were left over from the Depression and the war. The government's unimaginative reinforcement of Britain's already outdated economic structure meant that most of the political energy of the era was invested in the building of the welfare state. It turned out that the Beveridge Report was to be a much truer indicator of the impulses of post-war British society than was the Labour Party's historic program for nationalization and socialism. The suffering of the Depression and the war years had created a yearning for universal social services that would confer both dignity to all and a basic level of income, health care and housing. The National Insurance and National Assistance schemes were to provide income for those out of work and sick as well as paying out old age pensions. The National Health Service, which came into effect in July 1948, was to provide uniform health care to all without any payment to be later refunded — in contrast to the system in other countries. In fact, the National Health Service was to symbolize the whole post-war era, both at the time and later on. It was regarded as the triumphant cornerstone of a more egalitarian way of life by its supporters. Its detractors reviled it, claiming that it led to shoddy, demoralized health care service and often caused lengthy delays in essential surgery.

Even though the main governmental impulse in post-war Britain involved the development of the welfare state, there was some inclination in both major political parties to follow the interventionist example of countries like France. In 1961, under the inspiration of the French Plan, the Conservative government of Harold Macmillan established the National Economic Development Council, known as NEDDY. The body was not a government ministry but rather a forum in which business leaders, trade unionists and government officials could exchange long-range perspectives on the direction of the economy. Its activities were a watered- down version of what was happening across the Channel in Europe.

When the Labour Party was elected with Harold Wilson as Prime Minister in 1964, the notion of planning became more important still. A Department of Economic Affairs was established to oversee long-term economic development. The new department was intended to share power over the economy with the Treasury, from which fiscal and monetary policies emanated. In practice, the relationship between the two departments was uneasy and the new department never succeeded in elaborating a coherent vision on which the government acted. Britain's short-lived planning vogue was over by 1970 with the defeat of Harold Wilson by the Conservatives under Ted Heath. In the 1970s, Britain was to enter a difficult economic period, marked by slow growth and social conflict. In the end the post-war political consensus had not extended much past the welfare state. Economic planning of the kind pursued in the rest of Western Europe and Japan was not undertaken. Moreover, the social conflicts of the 1970s were to erode the centre ground on which the consensus had rested, thereby opening the door to the polarization that was to follow the election of Margaret Thatcher as Prime Minister in 1979.

Before we examine the radically altered economic and social policies of the Thatcher era, we need to assess Britain's economic record in the years after 1945 from two quite different perspectives — one internal to the country itself, and one comparing Britain to the rest of the industrialized world. Judged from the first perspective, Britain's post-war performance was a considerable success, while from the second, it was a deepening failure. During the 1950s and 1960s, the British economy grew more rapidly than at any time in its history. The result was a steady, and appreciable, growth in the incomes of the British people. For the twenty-year period from 1953 to 1973, growth in the British Gross Domestic Product (GDP), minus inflation, averaged 3 per cent a year. This compared very favourably with earlier periods in British history: 1856- 1873 — 2.2 per cent, 1873-1913 — 1.8 per cent, and 1924-1937 — 2.2 per cent. The comfortable rate of post- war real growth allowed Britain to develop the welfare state on the basis of a fairly wide consensus in British politics, including moderates in both major political parties. However, when we compare the British rate of growth with growth rates elsewhere for the same period, we can see how the British economy was headed, in the long run, for severe problems in terms of international competitiveness. During the period 1953-1973, the real growth rate in other European countries averaged as follows: France 5.3 per cent; West Germany 5.5

per cent; Italy 5.3 per cent; and Austria 5.7 per cent.[5] While the much higher growth rates on the continent in the immediate post-war years could be explained as the initial catch-up of war-torn nations rebuilding, later on this explanation became inadequate. The continental nations did not merely catch up with Britain, they soared past, achieving living standards much higher than those in the island nation. Most telling was Britain's faltering record of productivity growth in comparison to other advanced industrial nations. The problem was that increasing productivity abroad undermined the competitiveness of Britain's key industries.

During the period before 1973, more rapid economic growth and productivity growth in other countries posed only a potential threat to Britain. While it was true that British living standards were falling behind those in other countries, they were still increasing, and unemployment remained within reasonable bounds. After 1973, however, all this changed. The chronic problems facing Britain became acute. The manufacturing sector of the British economy, a pillar of the nation's very survival since the beginning of the industrial revolution, entered a period of absolute decline. In 1973, the index for British manufacturing stood at 114.6. From there output fell almost steadily until it reached 100 in 1980.[6] As the output of British manufacturing declined, there was a very sharp drop in manufacturing employment. In 1974, 7.87 million people were employed in British manufacturing; by 1981 this had dropped to 6.04 million.[7] While some other nations experienced a decline in the number of workers employed in manufacturing, no other nation replicated the severe drop in employment registered in Britain. Moreover, by 1980 the downward trend had been underway for twenty years.

The Thatcher Years

At the end of the 1970s, Britain elected a government with a bold vision for arresting the country's economic decline. That vision called for rolling back the welfare state in favour of a revival of a more slimmed down, classical capitalism. In the now desperate need to be competitive internationally, Britain would return to the economic philosophy that had made it great originally. Thatcherism, the vision of Britain's most forceful prime minister since Churchill, is an amalgam of classical liberalism and monetarism. Its essential idea is that the unfettered marketplace alone can restore the British economy to health. Margaret Thatcher came to office with one overriding idea for how this aim was to be achieved — by cutting public spending. The public sector must be cut down in size so that the private sector could acquire the room to do the job. To this end, firms must be allowed to fail if they must; the British economy must be forced to face foreign competition; and British workers must be forced to face up to reality when it came to making wage demands, if necessary by understanding that unemployment was the alternative.

If at the heart of Thatcherism there lay the simple economics of cutting back government spending, the politics was rather more complex. Margaret Thatcher had contempt both for the tory paternalists and the trade union leadership around whom the consensus of the postwar era had been formed. She did not look down on trade in favour of the refinement of the aristocracy. Rather she found the noblesse oblige of the old toryism effete and she intended to replace it with a harsh meritocracy. Her key constituency was the rising white collar suburbs of the relatively prosperous southeast of England and she knew how to appeal to its interests. In the 1979 election campaign, her promise to sell publicly owned council houses to their tenants at low prices was decisive to her victory. Later, she would deploy the same strategy in privatization of publicly owned corporations, putting them on the market at a low price so that those who purchased shares were bound to make a profit. It did not matter that neither of these moves had any impact on economic efficiency and that both of them amounted to selling short the interests of the taxpayers as a whole on behalf of a specific section of taxpayers. The point was to widen the base of support for a new kind of politics.

One aspect of the new politics was a sharp departure from the previous practice of seeking consensus among the major interest groups in the country. Margaret Thatcher regarded the quest for consensus as a sign of weakness. In a caustic response to criticisms from her predecessor Ted Heath, Thatcher stated: "To me, consensus seems to be the process of abandoning all beliefs, principles, values and policies.... It is the process of avoiding the very issues that have got to be solved merely to get people to come to an agreement on the way ahead."[8] This tough-minded stance was more than a personal idiosyncrasy. It was the means by which a radical transformation of British society could be achieved. If the market was to be restored to its rightful place, the welfare state would have to be cut back and British trade union power would have to be overcome. The old upper class tories, who valued stability ahead of the market, would never have pursued such goals.

If the politics of Thatcherism had an electric effect on Britain through the ending of the post-war consensus, the Thatcher government promptly fell flat on its face in its execution of economic policy. In 1979, the government embarked on a monetarist course with its key goals being to cut the growth of the money supply and to cut the Public Spending Borrowing Requirement (PSBR). While the policy did succeed in reducing British inflation, to 4.2 per cent by 1987, the consequences for employment and manufacturing output were dramatically negative. Unemployment, centred in the industrial north, Scotland and Wales, increased from 5.3 per cent in 1979 to 12.9 per cent in 1983, from which it declined to 10.5 per cent in 1987. Steel production sank by nearly 50 per cent from 1979 to 1980, from which slow recovery began but at levels far below those of the 1970s. Automobile production dropped as well, continuing the decline which had begun in the 1970s.[9]

Industrial decline heavily affected traditional sectors such as shipbuilding, once a mainstay of British prowess. The drastic decline of shipyards in Glasgow and the north of England bore eloquent testimony to the shift of the industry outside the United Kingdom. While in the years just prior to World War I, British shipyards had accounted for two- thirds of the world's production, by 1936 it was down to 36 per cent, by 1952 to 30 per cent and by 1986 to a paltry 1 per cent.

Declining output and employment were linked to the nation's negative balance of trade in secondary products. In 1983, Britain recorded a deficit in its trade in manufactured products for the first time since the Second World War, when the country had been heavily dependent on imported weapons and machinery. This was a major historic milestone. For the nation that had begun the industrial revolution to import more manufactured products than it exported was evidence indeed of change. While in 1972, Britain had a manufacturing trade surplus of L1688 million, in 1983 this had become a deficit of L2501 million, and in 1984 a deficit of L3647 million.

Faced with the plunge in manufacturing activity, the Thatcher government then claimed success in improving British productivity in the years of the most severe decline. In fact, what was occurring was that many of the less productive firms were simply going out of business, so that by definition, those that remained, on average, had to have higher productivity. The world would indeed be a simpler place if the road to greater efficiency just involved shutting down the less productive enterprises and then pointing to the misleading statistical gains in productivity that resulted. What was happening, of course, was that the manufacturing sector — one of the historic pillars on which the strength of the British economy had rested — was being allowed to crumble.

While manufacturing was in sharp decline, there were two other sectors to turn to: services, the key one being banking, insurance and finance; and North Sea oil.

Under Thatcher, British prosperity has centred on the global financial services of the City of London. There is no denying success in this sector. The City of London handles currency flows worth tens-of-billions of dollars a day. Micro-electronics makes possible instantaneous global financial transactions and the City of London is at their heart. In it is a greater concentration of global financial expertise than anywhere else. Still, the picture is not entirely rosy. Nothing could be more footloose than the financial industry. The very micro-electronic revolution which has heightened the historic role of the City of London could equally lead to a shift to other centres in other parts of the world, the most likely one being Tokyo, already the world's largest equity market in 1987.

If the future of the City of London is a matter for debate, one thing is not — the inability of the financial industry to bring sustained economic growth to Britain as a whole. In fact, the financial industry of London shows little interest in the manufacturing sector. There is nothing new in this — there has long been tension between British industry and the City of London; the British financial industry pre-dated the industrial revolution, and operating from its square mile in the City, it was much happier to lend money to finance global trade, much of which never touched Britain's shores, than it was to lend money to help re-tool British industry. While, during the post-war period, Japanese and West German banks, often under the direction of government economic strategies, channelled investment into industry, this was not the case in Britain. To a greater extent than elsewhere, British industrialists were forced to reinvest their own profits, unable to borrow from their national banks in the way that their foreign counterparts could. During the Thatcher era, the division between a world-class financial centre and a distressed national manufacturing sector has been very marked. While the City of London controls much of the savings of the British people, the bankers do not feel there is any reason to help rebuild British industry. And, according to the market nostrums of the Thatcher Conservatives, there is no particular reason why they should.

With British industry in sharp decline, the revenues realized from the production of North Sea oil were an immense stroke of good fortune. By the mid-1980s, petroleum activity accounted for about 8 per cent of Britain's Gross Domestic Product (GDP). In addition, it was petroleum revenues that prevented the country from having to choose between a sharp decline in living standards and a severe balance of payments crisis as a result of the manufacturing trade deficit.

Unfortunately, however, North Sea oil is a bounty with a distinctly limited potential. Oil and natural gas output have been projected to decline from a peak in the mid-1980s until Britain becomes, as it was before the mid-1970s, once again a net importer of petroleum sometime in the 1990s. The country will then face the prospect of even starker choices than at present. To date the impact of the decline of the manufacturing sector has been softened by North Sea Oil. What will happen when North Sea oil production declines?

As with Reaganism in the United States, Thatcherism involves one sphere where public sector spending is regarded with favour — national defence. In the 1980s, defence spending as a proportion of the Gross Domestic Product (GDP) was higher in Britain (5.4 per cent) than in Japan (1.0 per cent) or West Germany (3.4 per cent). In fact, it was second only to the United States (6.6 per cent) among the major countries in the non-communist world.[10] Even more important, a much higher proportion of the British research and development financed by government is defence-related than is the case in Japan or West Germany.[11] While British R and D spending as a whole was declining in the 1980s, the proportion of it devoted to defence was increasing. In 1983, Britain devoted .66 per cent of its GDP to defence- related research and development, second among capitalist nations only to the U.S. at .76 per cent, and far ahead of West Germany at .11 per cent, Italy at .04 per cent, and Japan at .01 per cent.[12]

Politically, Thatcher has performed brilliantly in the 1980s. True, without the Falklands War of 1982, her government would have had a much more difficult time winning re-election the following year. Yet, in the elections of 1983 and 1987 she showed clearly that political nimbleness — and not merely luck — accounts for her electoral success. In both campaigns, she was in contention against an enfeebled opposition, a Labour Party which was poorly led in 1983, and which attempted to defend the unpopular policy of unilateral nuclear disarmament in 1987. Splitting the opposition vote was the Liberal-Social Democrat (SDP) Alliance. Working against these foes, Margaret Thatcher stuck to her strengths, appealing to her constituency in the more affluent southeast of the country. The result in both elections was stunning victory. Thatcher can now boast of three consecutive majority governments, something not accomplished by any other British prime minister in this century.

But the victories have had costs — an increasingly bitter political atmosphere and a divided society. Even the supporters of Margaret Thatcher readily acknowledge that her policies have widened the gap between the rich and the poor in Britain. The conservative *Economist* wrote candidly: "Who has gained most from eight years of Thatcherism? The answer is unambiguously the better off ... wage differentials have widened: the lowest ten per cent of male earners have had a real pay increase of only four per cent; the top ten per cent of 22 per cent."[13] Conservative American columnist George F. Will, in the aftermath of the third Thatcher electoral victory, wrote: "Since Mrs. Thatcher came to power in 1979, inequality has increased. This is central to her program. Thatcherism is, aggressively, a meritocratic antidote to decades of egalitarianism."[14]

In the foregoing discussion, we have been examining particular aspects of the British economic paralysis. However, each of these aspects raises the deeper question "why?." Why the entrepreneurial failure, why the stubbornness of the unions, why the poor record of investment and of R and D? Taken together, these particular problems should be seen as symptoms of a deeper social failure.

The explanations for all of the particular problems tend to merge into a larger explanation of the underlying condition of British society. Indeed, what accounts for the particular problems and what unifies them is the failure to move beyond the assumptions on which British society operated during the era of its world power. It is the ideology of the market system itself which holds the key to the British crisis. As noted, British industrial society achieved its characteristic form in the early 19th century when the system of mercantilism was overturned in favour of the system of the free market. Both mercantilism and laissez-faire operated within a capitalist mode of production, but the shift was nonetheless a momentous one. It involved the adoption of a new set of assumptions in British society about the market, the state, capital and labour. The economic paradigm remained intact despite the rise of trade unionism, the challenge of Keynesianism and the emergence of the welfare state. Only in Britain, the United States and other English-speaking countries is the model of the market-driven economy the major, and only really legitimate, reference for economic practice. In turning to Thatcherism to deal with their economic crisis, the British were returning to the truths of 19th century laissez-faire. It is difficult to be reassured about the future social peace and prosperity of their country.

Chapter Four

What Has Japan Done?

In recent decades Japan has achieved greater success in climbing the ladder of international competitiveness than any other country. In the fall of 1986, Japan passed the United States in per capita Gross Domestic Product (GDP), an extraordinary achievement for a country that was devastated by the Second World War, with a per capita GDP only half that of the U.S. as late as the 1960s. In the late 1980s, Japan has become the leading lender of international capital, with 25 per cent of all loans from one country to another funded from Japan. Four of the five largest banks in the world are headquartered in Tokyo. Japan's massive trade surplus with the rest of the world and, in particular, with the United States, along with the very high savings of the Japanese themselves indicates that the country will become an ever greater lender of international capital. Japan, already a leading industrial power, is becoming as well the world's most important banker and foreign investor. It is especially in this latter development that Japan is challenging the role of the United States in the global economy.

Despite all these achievements, however, Japan's position in the global economy remains highly vulnerable. Its superb industrial exporting machine was slowed down appreciably in early 1987 when the skyrocketing yen (150 to the dollar), began pricing Japanese industrial products, most notably steel, out of world markets. Japanese unemployment climbed to 2.9 per cent, a highly desirable rate for most countries, but not for Japan where lifetime employment has been a key feature of high worker morale in major enterprises. Japan's much prized prowess at phasing down "sunset" industries such as steel in favour of "sunrise" industries such as semi-conductor devices and robots, was subjected to severe strains. Unprecedented layoffs occurred in the Japanese steel industry.

The fact is that Japan has learned how to master the post- war international economic system more effectively than any other country. But for all their achievements, the Japanese have not constructed a fireproof house. In fact, by the late 1980s, their own future economic growth is in doubt as a result of the crisis in the American designed post-war economic order, a crisis which Japanese economic success has done a great deal to create.

Birth of a Giant

To understand the problems Japan now faces as a result of its own success, we need to examine how and why the Japanese economy developed the way it has.

Considerable scholarship has been devoted to why Japan embarked on a course of rapid capitalist economic development in the late 19th century in contrast to the neighbouring countries in East Asia during that era. Was it because of the virtual revolution in Japanese economic policies implemented in the aftermath of the Meiji restoration of 1868? Alternatively, was it due to the economic and cultural inheritance of the Tokugawa period which preceded the Meiji era, and, among other things, brought the general level of Japanese education up to a relatively high level for a pre-industrial society?[1] Analysts have propounded both of these explanations, some giving them equal weight.[2] It is not our purpose here to enter into this debate, but simply to note its existence before examining the pace and nature of Japanese economic development.

During the crucial Meiji era, from 1868 to 1911, the country took the essential, coordinated steps toward modernization. A central bank, a sound and uniform currency, railways connecting the main centres, telegraph lines, imported western machinery — Japan, over a very short period of time, established an economic infrastructure and modern system of commerce, with the privately owned joint-stock company as its key operating unit. A late industrializing country, Japan was able to telescope dramatically these early stages of industrial development compared with the time it had taken early industrializing countries such as Britain and the United States to accomplish the same things.

What is more, these steps were taken not by business alone, but by business in conjunction with the state. What was occurring was a conscious strategy to put an entire system into place very rapidly. Here there was no laissez-faire, no following of the unseen hand of the market system. Largely because of the threat of western imperial intervention in Japan, business and government there were galvanized into acting together to spare their country the fate of ending up in some foreign country's empire, a fate which befell most of the countries of east Asia.

Because what was being undertaken was both a capitalist and national effort, the government was deeply involved from the beginning. It alone could organize Japan's effort to overcome backwardness. The state took the main role in putting the infrastructure — railways, telegraph systems and port facilities into place. It also set up model factories which imported western technology, and then, once Japanese business was ready, transferred them to private ownership. In this early period, and indeed right down to the Second World War, the Japanese government was by far the largest investor in the economy. Its share of domestic capital formation was sustained at over 40 per cent of the whole.[3] Economist Yoshihara Kunio summarizes the government's role in early Japanese industrial development this way:

> The difference between what the government wanted and what the private sector could accomplish was made more acute by the threat of Western imperialism. Having seen how Japan's neighbour, China, had been victimized by the Western Powers, the Meiji leaders were convinced of the need for military modernization and for building up the supporting economy. If Japan were to avoid China's fate, both military modernization and economic development had to be carried out immediately. Since the response of the private sector was expected to be slow and limited in scope, the government was forced to play an active role as educator, institutional innovator, and financier.[4]

During the Meiji period, rapid growth was only achieved by the 1880s, and it centred on the take-off of the cotton textile industry. By the beginning of the following decade, the textile industry, which was being quickly mechanized, began exporting its products, and had even established an overseas Japanese-owned mill in Shanghai in 1911. Rapid mastery of the technology, soon followed by exports and then by foreign investments — it was a cycle that was to be repeated many times in the future by Japanese industry.

The next period in Japanese development, from the eve of the First World War to the mid-1930s, saw the growth of the light industries which were geared for large-scale exports. Yet, even though light industries, textiles being the most important, were at the centre of Japan's manufacturing sector, heavy industry also grew, both at the beginning and end of this period. In both cases, it was military and political factors which spurred the development. During the First World War, Japan, an ally of Great Britain, had to develop its own capacity to produce machinery because the war effort absorbed all the industrial products that the western powers could turn out and they could no longer export capital goods to Japan. Following the war, Japanese manufacturing fell on hard times and machinery production was only sustained by raising tariffs. This was the era in which Japan relied increasingly on its own colonial empire, modelled very much on those of the western powers. Taiwan and Korea, both Japanese colonies, were expected to export food to Japan and were discouraged from developing their own industries, instead being expected to serve as markets for Japanese industrial exports.

This was also the era in which the concentration of Japanese industry in the hands of a few gigantic family-controlled combines reached its peak. Some of these combines — zaibatsu — pre-dated the era of the Meiji reforms. It was in the inter-war years, however, that the combines, which operated through holding companies to control operations in finance, industry and mining, achieved their greatest power. The most prominent zaibatsu were Mitsubishi, Mitsui and Sumitomo.[5] The ascendancy of the zaibatsu and their tendency to move into heavy industry was intimately connected with the rise of Japanese militarism in the 1930s. the zaibatsu profited from and were instrumental in the transition to virtual military rule.

The power of the zaibatsu continued to soar during the war itself, so that by its end the four largest family business empires controlled 50 per cent of the nation's finance, 32 per cent of its heavy industry and 11 per cent of its light industry.[6] While the first years of the war saw an increase in Japanese economic output, by its end the destruction of the country and its industrial plant was devastating. By August 1945, industrial production was down to a fraction of what it had been a year earlier; food production was down 30 per cent; an acute housing shortage in the cities was the legacy of the bombing; and the country had lost its overseas empire, the source of important raw materials for Japanese industry.

Post-war recovery was not easy. In the end, of course, it was accomplished and Japan began the economic expansion which was to become both a "miracle" and a major source of the crisis that has plagued the American-designed international economic system since the early 1970s.

In the immediate post-war years, Japan experienced hyper-inflation, its consumer price index soaring by 8,000 per cent from 1945 to 1949.[7] However, despite the inflationary chaos, industrial production began to grow again in Japan, by 1948 reaching half of the level of the mid-1930s, while at the same time food production once again reached the normal levels of the past.[8] In 1949, the Japanese government took steps to bring inflation under control, fixing the exchange rate of the yen at 360 to the dollar. Real takeoff, however, began only when the Korean War broke out in June 1950. This new war brought an economic boom in which demand for Japanese goods and services soared.

Japanese economic development in the early post Second World War period was crucially shaped by two factors: U.S. policy toward Japan; and the economic strategy of the Japanese government.

At first, the U.S. government was concerned only to maintain minimal living standards in Japan to avoid starvation and social chaos. Soon, however, the winds of geo-political transformation drastically changed the American attitude. The Cold War era of hostility between the U.S. and the Soviet Union had begun; by mid-1948, it seemed probable that the Communists would win the civil war in China. Under these vastly altered circumstances, Japan began to look like a potential political and economic buttress for American power in East Asia. American authorities assisted Japan with a supply of necessary raw materials and pushed for Japanese re-industrialization. By the time of the Korean War, American policy strongly endorsed rapid Japanese industrial growth. In September 1951, the San Francisco Peace Conference was convened and the treaty signed there led to the formal ending of the American military occupation of Japan the following spring.

Before going on to analyse the post-occupation period, we should take note of how American occupation policy helped to shape the character of the Japanese economy. American occupying authorities took steps to alter the political and economic systems in Japan. In the political realm, the Meiji constitution, defining the emperor as supreme ruler of the country, was scrapped in favour of a new constitution which made Japan a constitutional monarchy with a system modelled on that of the western democracies. On the economic front, the Americans intervened as well to create a competitive market economy in Japan. As they had in West Germany, the Americans enforced the break-up of Japanese cartels. The holdings of the zaibatsu were divided up by the Holding Company Liquidation Commission, set up in 1946 — eighty-three holding companies and fifty-seven zaibatsu families were forced to give up their conglomerate ownerships.[9]

The break-up of the zaibatsu by no means ended the operations of the individual companies that had been held by them; on the contrary, in the years to come, many of these companies were to achieve great success. And indeed, as the American attitude to Japan changed, the early emphasis on breaking up large concentrations of corporate power gave way before U.S. determination to revive Japanese industrial strength. By the time of the Korean War, the U.S. attitude to Japanese enterprise had changed dramatically. As economist Michio Morishima has written: "As a result of this shift Japanese capitalism re-emerged like a phoenix in a form almost identical to that of the prewar period.... An economy revived which once again had as its nucleus large enterprises. Over the five year period starting in 1950, Japanese enterprises were enriched by the huge demand for military commodities to be used in the Korean War by American forces."[10]

Thanks to the about-face in American policy, large enterprises boomed, particularly the steel and machine tool producers. Within a decade of the dissolution of the zaibatsu, large-scale enterprises once again were dominant in Japanese economic life. To be sure, the old families never got back their former economic power. Instead a new managerial elite emerged to run the pre-eminent enterprise groups — Mitsubishi, Mitsui and Sumitomo — along quite different lines. The large companies did not control as much of the economy as had their predecessors. And the companies held by the large conglomerates had much more managerial independence than under the old zaibatsu.[11] It would not be inaccurate to say that the old system of family-run cartels had been replaced by a system of oligopolistic enterprises, operating in a competitive framework and run by a managerial elite.

The Japanese Model

If the altered structure of business in Japan was to be a key to the success of the economy, so too was the economic strategy of the Japanese government, and the means it employed to pursue that strategy. From the end of the war to the present day, Japan has consistently adhered to a policy of government intervention in the country's economic life. Such intervention has not negated the market economy. Rather, it has directed industry toward particular long-range goals, steering it away from others — promoting competition in some cases, while restricting it where its effects have been seen as potentially destructive. As economist Ryutaro Komiya described it: "Industrial policy is government policy that changes the allocation of resources among industries, or the levels of certain types of production among firms within individual industries. It is designed to encourage production, investment, research and development, modernization and reorganization in some industries and not in others."[12]

Japan's post-war strategy set out, in defiance of conventional economic theory, to concentrate on the building of capital intensive industries rather than labour intensive ones — despite the fact that Japan was a country with a surplus of labour. Reflecting on this crucial choice, a Japanese vice-minister for International Trade and Industry said that it was "decided to establish in Japan industries which required intensive employment of capital and technology, industries that in consideration of comparative costs of production should be the most inappropriate for Japan, industries such as steel, oil refining, petrochemicals, automobiles, aircraft, industrial machinery of all sorts, and electronics including electronic computers. From a short-run, static viewpoint, encouragement of such industries would seem to conflict with economic rationalism. But from a long-range viewpoint, these are precisely the industries where ... demand is high, technological progress is rapid, and labour productivity rises fast."[13]

In the post-war decades the crucial instrument of government intervention was the Ministry of International Trade and Industry (MITI). Yet, while MITI was the key agency in implementing Japanese industrial strategy, it was never an all-powerful body which handed down it fiats to the private sector. Although it has had specific powers which at times it has used to the full, MITI's approach has been to work with private companies, and with unions and other bodies, to attempt to achieve a consensus about the general direction of the economy and specific subsectors within it. In December 1985, I attended a consensus-making forum in Tokyo at which MITI officials were meeting with company executives and union leaders to hash out some problems in a specific industrial sector. The meeting was just one of many to work out a strategy. When the process had been completed, implementation would be easy since all the major players had had a part in reaching the decision.

In the early 1950s, MITI concluded that Japan's future depended on a shift from the light industries (textiles, in particular) which had been dominant in the past, to heavy industries. It set out both to coordinate the change, convincing business leaders of the need for it, and to use its powers to make the transition possible. Because it was operating in an economy in which foreign exchange and foreign technology were scarce resources, MITI used control over these to foster the change it wanted in the national economy. It used its powers to allocate foreign exchange, raw materials and foreign technology to assist firms in the development of heavy industry. It initiated loans at favourable rates from the Japan Development Bank. It underwrote specific ventures with special tax incentives and with special allowances for losses.

MITI also intervened to prevent too much capital from flowing into specific sectors, by suspending offers of inducements and, in some cases, even by withholding the necessary licenses to operate. Its intention here was to ensure that the firms undertaking favoured projects would be successful, and for this reason it was ready to act, if necessary, to prevent too many firms from rushing into the sector. The agency also took steps in some cases to deny foreign exchange to importers in order to lessen competition with domestic industry. Economist Yoshihara Kunio has explained how MITI coordinated development in complementary fields to make sure that investments were balanced:

> ....if a steel company had an expansion project which would result in too large an increase in supply, it was told to scale down the expansion project, or the users of the steel were encouraged to step up their investments in order to use more steel ... if a company wanted to set up a refinery in a complex, MITI could persuade an electric power company to set up a plant (which would use heavy oil from the refinery as fuel) and a chemical company to set up an ethylene factory (which would use naphtha from the refinery) in the complex. The ethylene factory would, in turn, be assured of factories which would use ethylene to produce various chemical compounds.[14]

To help companies through difficult periods, MITI was empowered to set up cartels on a temporary basis. Companies involved in such cartels were required to come to a mutual pricing arrangement to ensure survival for each of the members. Once the recession or market turndown had passed, the cartel was dissolved.

Naturally MITI's success did not flow from its structure and approach alone. It was based as well on the agency's remarkable effectiveness at winning over the country's entrepreneurs — establishing a relationship of trust with them and involving them in its process and decisions. In this respect MITI's personnel was similar to that of the Plan in France in the post-war period (see Chapter 6). In the case of both MITI and the Plan an energetic and zealous group of bureaucrats, with high morale and obvious talent, were able to motivate the private sector as well as draw up a framework within which development would take place.

The agency did not always get its way, however, nor were its plans always brilliantly thought out and uniformly successful. Economists Yutaka Kosai and Yoshitaro Ogino have written about one such MITI failure: "In 1955 the Ministry of International Trade and Industry decided that there were too many producers in the car industry, so that production was on too small a scale. They came up with the idea of amalgamating them into one national company. This did not, of course, materialize, but in 1961 they tried, again unsuccessfully, to reduce the number of companies to just three."[15]

Despite mistakes, MITI lent Japanese economic development a strategic character, helping it to attain difficult, but highly desirable goals. The results were not immediate, but were impressive nonetheless. For example, the shift from light to heavy industry, begun in the mid-1950s, took a decade to pay full dividends. At first, the transition was costly and it was unclear whether the necessary export markets would materialize and make the change viable. Indeed, it took until 1960 for Japanese exports to return to their pre-World War II level. (Japan's overall imports exceeded exports until 1964, and until that date, the country ran a trade deficit with the United States.)[16] From 1960 to 1973 Japanese exports expanded sevenfold. As Yoshihara Kunio concludes: "In this process of rapid overall expansion textile products, which had been so important in the pre-war period, became insignificant, whereas the heavy industrial goods, previously unimportant or non-existent came to dominate."[17] By the early 1960s, Japanese industry had become a world leader in the production of passenger cars, synthetic fibres, steel, petrochemicals and electronic goods.

Two other examples where MITI played a role in advancing the competitive position of the Japanese economy were: computers and microchips; and industrial robots. In the 1960s, Japan was distinctly inferior — to the West in general and the United States in particular — in the development of computers. Under MITI's guidance, Japan set out to rectify this situation with results so spectacular that the international balance of advantage in microprocessing has been dramatically changed. In 1970, MITI published its overview of where the national economy should go, "The Vision for the 1970s." It stressed the crucial importance of knowledge-intensive industries and, in particular, of computers.[18] It called for a change in the Japanese economic effort that paralleled its strategy for the shift from light to heavy industry in the mid-1950s. Under MITI's guidance the following steps were taken:

- In 1971, a program called "the System of Subsidies for Promoting the Development of Computers" was launched through which conditional loans were made to companies to cover 50 per cent of the costs of the development of computers.

- For four years in the late 1970s, seventy-five billion yen, 40 per cent of it coming from the government, was spent on basic research for the promotion of the semi- conductor industry. The Very Large Scale Integrated Circuit (VLSI) research association, set up by MITI, provided Japanese producers with the means to pool this research effort and to share in its results. As the Organization for Economic Cooperation and Development (OECD) concluded: "The advantages of such cooperation are evident: every firm can learn from each other's mistakes, and the costs of research are much lower."[19] This cooperation among firms in basic research did not inhibit competition among them in the creation of their own distinctive final products. To back up its huge effort in the area of computer technology, the Japanese public sector practised a policy of discriminatory purchasing, favouring domestic computers and other semi-conductor devices. It also acted to inhibit imports so that a larger portion of the home market would be reserved for the domestic product.

This daring and wide-ranging approach enabled Japan to advance from being a net importer to a net exporter of computers by 1981. And from that point, progress continued to be very rapid. While 10.5 per cent of Japanese computers were exported in 1980, by 1983 34.7 per cent of them sold abroad.[20] In the half decade from 1978 to 1983, the Japanese share of the computer export market for all OECD countries increased from 5.2 per cent to 18 per cent — largely at the expense of Britain and West Germany, whose share of exports was falling.[21] Between 1975 and 1984, Japan's electrical machinery industry grew at 16.4 per cent a year. Even more remarkable, productivity in this sector in Japan increased at the rate of 13.2 per cent a year for the same period, compared with 4.5 per cent a year in the United States and 3.5 per cent a year in West Germany.[22] By the time the rest of the world woke up to what had happened, the Japanese had taken over a very large chunk of the world market for computers and microchips.

By 1983, although the United States remained the world's largest producer of electronic products, that country had become a net importer of them.[23] The confident assumption expressed by many Americans, that while the Japanese may have learned to produce cars efficiently, the high-tech future belonged to the United States, had been shattered. Once the Japanese electronics revolution had been completed, Europeans and Americans were inclined to cry foul on the grounds that it had not been accomplished through the operations of the market alone. They were right. It was a planned assault on the technological high-ground, carried out by Japanese government and industry working together. By 1987, the United States was shifting uneasily between quests for a "peace treaty" with the Japanese in this sector, to prevent the further erosion of the American electronics industry, and a protectionist crusade to push Japan out of sensitive parts of the domestic market.

The Japanese computer breakthrough was closely related to the development of industrial robots. Here again MITI played a key role, coordinating research into the development of robots. Low interest loans and attractive depreciation allowances were made available to encourage companies to switch to the use of robots in their production facilities. In addition, MITI, the robot manufacturers and the Japan Development Bank sponsored a scheme to allow small companies to use robots. Because small businesses are not normally in a position to purchase expensive industrial products, the plan made it possible to rent them. In 1985, I visited the Mitsubishi robot-rental showroom in Tokyo. The facility features a range of industrial robots, each with specific capabilities. Technical staff teach visiting businesspeople how to operate the robots and to decide which ones are appropriate for them.

Making high tech accessible to all of Japanese business has been a key MITI goal. The showroom I visited is an example of how the goal is met. Assessing Japan's performance the OECD pointed to "a very highly developed, publicly- promoted system of industrial standardization which promotes the diffusion of technical information from large to small enterprises."[24]

In the mid-1980s, about half the industrial robots in the world were deployed in Japan. In 1983, 16,500 robot units were in operation in Japanese industry compared with 8,000 in the United States, 4,800 in West Germany, and 1900 in Sweden. For every 10,000 manufacturing workers Japan had deployed thirteen robots, putting it well ahead of the United States where there were only four robots for every 10,000 workers, but behind Sweden where the ratio was almost thirty robots to 10,000 workers.[25]

Numbers such as this tell us that robots, a key to the manufacturing of the future, are only beginning to work their transformation of the world's industries. Driven by computers, industrial robots are quickly replacing workers on industrial assembly lines — most notably in the automotive sector. Human beings simply cannot compete with robots when it comes to repetitive tasks. Moreover, robots are essential in the shift that is underway to flexible and customized manufacturing. As vehicles move along the assembly line, they can be dealt with individually by robots carrying out the instructions of a computer; different models, with different options, can be easily produced in this way on a single assembly line. In addition to production flexibility, the sheer labour saving potential of robots is awesome. Japan has gone further than the other major industrial countries in transforming its work force as a result of the introduction of robots.

To date, the impact of robots has been mainly in narrowly defined industrial areas. As stated, the automotive industry is the sector in which robot use is now widest, and here too, the impact so far is highly specific. By the mid-1980s, almost all spotwelding in auto plants was handled by robots. Soon painting and the surface treatment of car bodies will be entirely robotized.[26]

Let us summarize our comments to this point on MITI's role in coordinating Japanese industrial strategy. The agency has acted as a long-range strategist for the whole of the Japanese economy, in many cases offsetting the short-run tendencies of the market. Each of the large steps taken in moving the Japanese economy forward have involved strategic thinking on the part of MITI, and careful coordination of effort by the private and public sectors. If Japan had relied on signals from the market alone, it would not have taken the bold steps needed to restructure the economy. It was precisely the willingness to act well in advance of market demand, to take the necessary lead time to develop new industrial potential and new lines of products, that paid off. Then, when it came to selling their products in competition with both domestic and foreign companies, Japanese enterprises showed themselves adept at operating effectively in the market place.

In the last two decades, as Japan has overcome its shortage of raw materials and imported technology, some of MITI's powers have been curtailed. In part, this has been the result of Japan's success in overtaking the West. In the 1980s, the goals of Japan's economic strategy have been more diffuse and difficult to attain than in the past. They are centred on human development and adaptation in a society in which high technology has been growing ever more important. This involves planning the emergence of "sunrise" industries as well as planning for the phase-down of "sunset" industries.

The educational system is at the very centre of Japan's current economic strategy, the key to whether the Japanese people will be trained for and able to cope with the demands of their technological economy. The OECD has pointed out that the Japanese educational system has encouraged the broad diffusion of technological capabilities by ensuring "an abundant supply of 'medium trained' industrial manpower, with a strong emphasis on the engineering professions."[27] Japanese education also earned high praise from another quarter when the U.S. Department of Education took the unusual step of issuing a study of another country's system in early January 1987. The study depicted Japan as a "learning society of formidable dimensions" in which the relationship between the schools and the job market were "closer and more effective than in most other industrialized countries." U.S. secretary of education William J. Bennett wrote in his study that: "the Japanese generally seem to expect a level of performance that is closer to children's true intellectual capacities than Americans ordinarily do." In the same vein, the report pointed to two central assumptions that underlie Japanese education: "One is that virtually all children have the ability to learn well and to master the regular school curriculum. The second is that certain habits and characteristics, such as diligence and attention to detail, can be taught." The study noted that Japanese students have consistently achieved high results on international tests of educational accomplishment.[28]

The laudatory U.S. report on Japanese education was not reciprocated in a Japanese study of American education that was released in Tokyo at the same time. The chief author of the report, Isao Amagi, explained at a news conference why his study did not suggest that Japan emulate the American system:

> Recently, the outcome of math tests show Japanese kids scoring higher than Americans. American scholars have begun to question why. They know that Japanese class hours are longer than the Americans' and that Japanese schools are using the class hours more efficiently, and that Japanese teachers impose a lot of homework on kids.
>
> American scholars seen to share the view that the American educational system has fallen into mediocrity. American kids register very bad scores on international tests. In the past they talked of a 'sputnik shock'. Now maybe there's a 'Toyota shock'.[29]

Not everyone thinks the Japanese system is perfect. Critics have suggested that Japanese universities have a long way to go before they become world class institutions.[30] Others have warned that Japanese schools do little to promote originality and creativity in students. Finally, there is concern that the system is so competitive that it pushes some students past the breaking point and is contributing to a rising toll in human misery. Despite these criticisms, however, there is no doubt that Japanese education has succeeded in giving the country the depth in trained manpower needed to sustain the transformation to a society based on high technology.

Trained manpower, it is now evident, can only make its full contribution to economic growth in a society that values what workers as well as managers have to say. Here, too, Japan has led the way. The relationship between management and workers in major Japanese industries has been quite different from the norm in the West — and that difference has given Japan a competitive edge. It is difficult not to be impressed, even a little overawed, when one comes in contact with Japanese industrial management. When I met K. Tsukamoto, the Plant

Manager of the Okamoto machine-tool plant north of Tokyo, he was dressed in the same blue-collar outfit as the workers on the plant floor. While dressing like the rest of the work force is now standard practice for Japanese plant executives, what came as a real shock was that Mr. Tsukamoto had no office of his own. His desk was located on the plant floor next to the production unit. All of the office staff at the plant had their desks there, and naturally, they too were dressed in blue-collar work-clothes.

When I paid my visit the plant was experimenting with the elimination of all chairs for office workers, so that they stood at their desks, thus further cutting down any distinction between production and office staff. I suspected that this was not one of the great ideas of our time, and that the chairs might well return, a few dozen backaches down the line. But what mattered was the genuine effort to find ways to bring all parts of the work force and management together to keep morale high.

The Okamoto Plant, like many in the Japanese machinery industry, depends heavily on foreign markets, in this case mainly in the United States and China. Staying competitive in the international marketplace is very much on the minds of managers there, and apparently of the workers as well. The week before my visit, the production workers had met to complain that materials were not being streamed into the plant smoothly enough to allow maximum production to be achieved. They wanted things better organized at that end so that a big export order whose deadline was approaching could be met on time.

On the floor of the plant, some of the workers were clearly streamed for future management jobs. One of them was a graduate engineer who would work on the floor for three years, to master all of the details of the production process before going on to a management job. Companies such as Okamoto make a policy of recruiting their executives from within the company, a policy which heightens morale on the plant floor and makes it clear that hard work can open the door to advancement. The policy, of course, also ensures that a very high proportion of Japanese executives have "hands-on" production experience, in sharp contrast with the United States where executives tend to come from the "money" end of the business.

Japanese business goes to great lengths to ensure that top managers do not lose contact with the people who work for them. Executives are continually trained and retrained to keep their humanity alive. I visited one institution which exists for this purpose, the Kinrisha School south of Tokyo. The Kinrisha School is located in a collection of spartan-like residences in a hilly region with Mount Fuji making a spectacular backdrop. Students there — business executives or would-be executives, ranging in age from twenty to sixty — 95 per cent of them men, are divided into groups of eight to ten. They spend arduous fourteen hour days led by instructors through a program of chanting, reciting, singing, and physical exercises, including an all- night forty kilometer outing. Through North American eyes, the training appears bizarre in the extreme — a fantasy land of rote indoctrination. Actually what is happening is that the individualism of the students, their sense of being special and apart from those they work with and will supervise, is being broken down.

Japanese industry has been very successful at motivating workers, at instituting a system in which ideas on how best to do the job flow both ways between management and labour, and not simply from the top down. In part, this has been due to the "lifetime" employment guarantee given workers in most large companies. Knowing your job is there for life gives a worker not only security but pride in the company's products and a feeling of responsibility for how well the company does.

This is all in sharp contrast to the norm in American business, despite the trendy quest for "excellence" in recent years. American industry, under the sharp assault of competitive pressure from abroad, is only now beginning to turn away from the Frederick Taylor philosophy of "scientific management." This philosophy cares little about the long-run well-being of the work force, and is instead geared to getting as much out of employees as possible — in the short run.

The Japanese management philosophy, on the other hand, has grown out of a traditional cultural ethos and many of its features pre-date the modern industrial world. The practices of Japanese management are controversial in western countries, and there is good reason for this. In a broad sense, Japanese management can be described as paternalistic. Large Japanese companies provide much more than a lifetime place of work for their employees; the company is often the central focus of the social and recreational life of the worker. Companies thus inculcate a strong loyalty in their employees that is incomprehensible in the West. Through "Quality Circles," workers are often organized into small groups in which they can be involved in decisions about production. Normally, large companies make use of a seniority-graded wage system to reward and motivate workers. In addition to seniority based increases, workers can receive increases based on management evaluation.

Yoshihara Kunio has described the effect of the system as follows: "Job evaluation is a very important incentive to ordinary workers, as a good evaluation enables them to move up the wage scale, even if they continue to do the same work.... In the Western system, however, the range of wage increases without promotion, is limited. As a result, ordinary workers, most of whom continue to do the same work until retirement, generally have relatively low morale, and this affects corporate performance adversely."[31] He cites a comparison of the wage increases of manual workers at Hitachi and British Electric, both manufacturers of electrical equipment. In the late 1960s, the wages of a worker at Hitachi would have increased between 2.5 and 4.0 times during their careers from their late teens to their mid-fifties. In the case of British Electric, after age twenty-five, the manual worker had hardly any pay increase at all.[32]

It should be noted that this discussion of Japanese enterprise does not extend to small business. In Japanese small business, lifetime employment scarcely exists and wages are much lower than in the large firms. If Japan is noteworthy for the rapid introduction of robots on assembly lines, it is also noteworthy for perpetuating "cottage" industries, in which workers (usually women) toil at home for very low wages producing parts for vehicle interiors. Japan's rapid industrial rise has left it with a dual economy in which world competitive enterprises co-exist with and make use of labour-intensive sweat shops.

Through its industrial strategies, educational system, and corporate organization, Japan has made enormous progress in recent decades, doubling the size of its economy relative to that of the United States between 1960 and the mid-1980s. How well positioned is Japan in the late 1980s for the great battle for technological supremacy with the United States? The question is important because many Americans assume that in the end high technology, where most of the scientific breakthroughs to date have been made in the United States, will be their country's ultimate salvation. While the evidence on this issue will not be fully in for years, there are already important indications that in the deployment of high technology it is the Japanese, and not the Americans, who are winning the battle.

Take, for example, computer-based equipment and systems in manufacturing. Computer Integrated Machinery (CIM) utilizes robots and other computer controlled machines, linked together in a production system which is controlled by larger computers. By changing the guiding computer program, you can order the system to produce different goods. This revolutionizes manufacturing by allowing very great efficiency with very short production runs and allows companies to custom produce for their customers. It liberates manufacturing from the tyranny of the old- fashioned assembly line in which extremely long production runs of the same product were necessary to achieve the benefits of economies of scale.

If the deployment of flexible manufacturing systems is the key to competitiveness in the future, the Japanese appear to have a long lead already. A study by Professor Ramchandran Jaikumar, of the Harvard Graduate School of Business Administration, appeared in the *Harvard Business Review* in the fall of 1986. Professor Jaikumar studied thirty-five flexible manufacturing systems in the United States and sixty in Japan in 1984 — more than half the systems then in place in the two countries — and concluded that in comparison to Japan the United States ended up appearing like "a desert of mediocrity." He warned that "rather than narrowing the competitive gap with Japan, the technology of automation is widening it further."[33]

In his study, Professor Jaikumar noted that American companies tended not to take full advantage of the revolutionary potential of the new system — in marked contrast to their Japanese competitors. Instead of using the flexible potential to produce a large number of products, they tended to program their systems to produce long runs of only a few products. While the average number of parts turned out by an American flexible manufacturer was only ten, the average for a Japanese producer was ninety-three. Jaikumar estimated that in the past half-decade the Japanese have spent more than twice as much as the Americans on automated equipment, but he believes the greatest Japanese advantage comes from what he calls "technological literacy." More than 40 per cent of those who work in the Japanese companies he studied were graduate engineers, compared with only 8 per cent in the American companies. And while all of the workers in the Japanese plants had been trained to work with computer-controlled machinery, only a quarter of those in the American plants had been. The better-trained Japanese work teams were much more able to adapt and improve engineer-designed programs for producing goods than were those in the American work places.[34]

A second study, by five business school professors — two Americans, two Europeans and one Japanese — confirms the conclusions drawn by Jaikumar. Their study concluded that North American and western European industry was far behind its Japanese competitors in taking advantage of the cost- cutting benefits of rapid production and design changes that are made possible by computer-integrated machinery.[35]

Even though it is too early to tell just how the Japanese- American race for supremacy in high technology will turn out, it is not unreasonable to conclude that the momentum is on Japan's side in the general battle for improved industrial productivity and growth. The pattern of much slower American economic growth as compared with that of Japan has persisted throughout the post-war decades. Between 1950 and 1983 the American economy grew at an average rate of 3.25 per cent a year, while Japan grew at more than twice this pace — 7.87 per cent a year.[36] The result has been a revolution in the global economy. Japan, with its long-term strategic planning involving both the state and the private sector, has ascended to the zenith of industrial capability and it is now the Americans who are playing catch-up.

Japan's extraordinary success, however, has not come without cost to the global economic order and potentially to itself. Like West Germany, Japan has based its economic strength on enormous exports. While Japan requires very large imports of resources, the most important of which is petroleum, it has enjoyed a huge surplus in its trade with the other industrialized countries since the early 1960s. For example, in 1983, Japan's trade surplus with the United States was $19.3 billion, with West Germany $3.3 billion and with Britain $2.9 billion.[37] In 1984, Japan had an overall merchandise trade surplus of $44.4 billion; it imported $60.3 billion worth of petroleum and $19.2 billion worth of other resources, while exporting $59.9 billion in goods to the United States and $23.9 billion to western Europe. Almost all of these exports were manufactured products.[38] By 1986, Japan's overall trade surplus had reached $92 billion.[39] From the early 1960s on, Japan managed a surplus on its current account (balance of payments) of about 1 per cent of its GDP, excluding several years when very high oil prices wiped this out. By 1983, with the collapse of oil prices and the swelling Japanese trade surplus with other industrialized countries, the current account surplus had soared to about 3 per cent of GDP. What this meant was that a very large number of Japanese industrial jobs were now dependent on the country's ability to sustain very large trade surpluses with other industrialized countries and a huge balance of payments surplus with the rest of the world.

The problem was that Japan's trade surplus was the counterpart of an enormous American trade deficit, totalling $170 billion in 1986 ($60 billion of it with Japan). Japan had learned very well how to maximize its position in the American-designed global economy by running its gigantic trade surpluses. Unfortunately for this strategy, the United States was no longer the economic power it had once been and the international economic order it had erected was disintegrating. With the yen soaring in value in 1986 and Japanese industrial production actually registering a decline of 2.4 per cent for the last quarter of the year as a result,[40] Japan was clearly paying a price for its success. Up until now Japan has adapted brilliantly to the task of performing competitively in an economic system designed by another nation. Now, to hold onto the gains it has made, it will have to play a major role in reordering the global economic system.

Chapter Five

West Germany: What Kind of Market System?

There was a time when Americans felt a sense of fond parenthood for the new state of West Germany, with its political democracy and market economy. In the 1960s, West Germany was often called "little America" by admirers who were pleased with how well the country had followed in the path of its great mentor.

There is no doubt that the United States played a key role in the creation of West Germany and in shaping its social and economic evolution. In the longer term, however, America was presiding over the rise of a formidable economic competitor. By the mid-1980s, West Germany had surpassed the United States in key industrial fields, most notably the production of machinery and capital equipment. Indeed, it had passed the United States, a country with four times its population, as the biggest exporter of commodities in the world. And what mattered most to the West German people, the country's per capita GDP had pulled close to that of the United States, having started from a position of only 50 per cent of American per capita income in the early post-war years.

West Germany's strategy has placed it clearly within the category of the enterprise-intervention economies, but it has, without doubt, been the least interventionist of those countries. Despite West Germany's very solid reputation for economic success in the English-speaking world, the days of its most rapid growth are now long past. While West Germany did well vis-à-vis the United States, its growth rate did not keep pace with that of other major Western European nations — both Italy and France having achieved faster growth over the quarter-century from 1960 to the mid-1980s.

The Making of a Miracle

At the end of the Second World War, the policy of the major allied countries was to prevent Germany from ever again becoming an industrialized power with a potential for military action. The defeated country was divided into four zones. For a time, it appeared possible that there would be no "Germany" in the future, but rather a number of small states within which an agricultural economy with minimal industry would exist. But the growing Cold War division between the western powers and the Soviet Union decisively changed Germany's fortune. In 1947, the American and British occupation zones were united for economic and administrative purposes, and a year later the French zone was joined with them. In 1949, the Federal Republic of Germany (FRG) was established, while in the Soviet zone the German Democratic Republic (GDR) was created.

In the immediate post-war period there were competing political tendencies in what was to become West Germany. The devastation, the collapse of the economy, and the fact that many leading industrialists had been supporters of the former Nazi regime, contributed to a widespread anti- capitalist sentiment among ordinary Germans. Such divisions were soon submerged, however, as a result of what was to be the decisive influence in the shaping of the West Germany political economy — the determination of the United States to launch a free-market system in the country.

As the Cold War intensified, the American attitude to Germany evolved rapidly. From wanting the dismantling of German industry, the United States came to see western Germany as a potential bulwark against the Soviet Union, as a country whose industrial potential could be key to strengthening a capitalist western Europe. In this spirit, it was decided that Marshall Plan aid from the United States, used to help rebuild shattered western Europe, would be made available as well for what was to become West Germany. In the early 1950s, with the new federal republic already established, the Korean War accelerated the American desire for a reindustrialized West Germany and increased the American market for German machinery.

What was being launched was to become one of the most successful market economies ever — but we must note that it was to be a market economy with very important differences from that in the

United States. The key power nexus in designing the new German economy was the link between the American occupying authorities and the younger, more entrepreneurial elements in German business. German capitalism was to be reconstituted, but the old order, based on cartels which had parcelled out market shares in major industries, was to be abandoned in favour of a competitive industrial system. To make the wager for the market economy pay off against the old business elements who had wanted the cartels restored, what was needed was rapid and sustained economic growth.

Indeed, growth in the 1950s was to cement the new system in place. In considering just how crucial growth was to the success of West Germany, we can appreciate a basic sense in which the West German economy was to differ from the American. For Americans, the market system was its own justification, a bulwark of freedom and good economic sense — an end in itself. It did not have to be defended and nurtured as a "system." This was decidedly not the case in West Germany, where the market system would only succeed in holding the society together if it worked so well that potential opposition to it could be crushed.   That was why expansion was of the essence. Growth would win support for the system and give it longevity. Moreover, expansion was to be much more than the sum of the achievements of German entrepreneurs alone. It was a "systemic" achievement from the start and the system involved both private enterprise and the intervention of the state.   What also differentiated the German from the American model of market economy was the notion of co-determination of industry, involving workers as well as management. Although the anti-capitalism of German workers was largely overcome by the success of economic growth, the concept of co- determination rather than unfettered capitalism has become a major legacy for West German society. In the chaotic atmosphere of the late 1940s, with German industry threatened with de-concentration by the allies and by trade union agitation for working-class power, important industrialists, hoping to head off the threat, compromised and negotiated agreements for the introduction of an equal number of worker representatives on their supervisory boards.[1] Although trade union power waned in the early years of the federal republic, both because of the renewed confidence of industrialists and the hostility of the Americans to "socialist experiments," in 1951 the Bonn government, under the threat of strikes, passed a co- determination law. Under the law, enterprises in the coal and steel industries with a thousand or more employees were to have workers' representatives on their supervisory boards; each of these firms was to have a worker director on its board of directors.[2] The following year, a Works Constitution Act extended the concept of a decision-making input to workers in almost all firms in matters of social welfare and personnel. All this fell far short of the "workers' control" that trade unionists and social democrats had envisioned earlier, but it nonetheless significantly altered industrial relations in West Germany. It contributed to a non-adversarial style in labour- management relations and was one reason why West Germany was to have so few strikes compared with other western countries.[3]

The initial takeoff of the West German economy was aided by other factors unique to that period. These include:

- The arrival in the first post-war years of ten million German refugees from the east, a vast reinforcement of the country's labour force. This enormous influx of people, many of them highly skilled, helped keep German wages low during the 1950s.

- The turmoil that followed the war caused a turnover in the ranks of German entrepreneurs, pushing to the fore younger, more energetic people, who were prepared to embrace the new system of capitalism without cartels.

- Although destruction during the war had been very great, the military effort had also required a major expansion of the German industrial plant. Much of that industrial base was refurbished and put back into service relatively quickly.

West German growth in the 1950s was more rapid than in any earlier period in German history. The real GDP increased on average by 8 per cent per year during the decade. This growth, the fastest in Europe at that time, made West Germany's GDP the highest in Western Europe by 1960.[4] By then unemployment had also fallen to less than 1 per cent of the labour force, income per capita had more than doubled and the country's severe housing crisis had been substantially reduced.[5]

Along with growth went a dramatic alteration in the structure of the West German economy. Agricultural employment dropped from 25 to 14.5 per cent of the labour force during the 1950s, while heavy industry — chemicals, machinery, and automobile manufacturing —

became the key to expansion, accounting together for about 40 per cent of total employment.[6]

From the start a key feature of the West German economy was to be its export orientation. In fact, West Germany was to become the greatest export machine in the world, continuing to sell abroad a much higher proportion of its total output than did Japan throughout the post-war decades. By 1984, West Germany was exporting 31.1 per cent of its GDP as compared to 15.1 per cent for Japan.[7] The fact that the West German economy was built for exports was to be a determining factor in its future direction, giving it great strength in key fields, but also making it highly vulnerable to changes in world demand. The extremely high proportion of the country's GDP that was exported reinforced the determination of the country's political leadership to play down the interventionist features of West German economic life for fear of sparking protectionism in other countries.

Over the course of the 1950s, exports grew from 9 per cent to 19 per cent of GDP.[8] At the heart of West Germany's export-led economy were automobiles and machinery. For North Americans, the first inkling of what was to become a global economic revolution came when the Volkswagen Beetles rumbled ashore in large numbers in the late 1950s. By that time 33.7 per cent of West Germany's vehicles were being exported as was 29.2 per cent of the country's production in machinery.[9]

American pressure for German industrialization was reinforced by the policies of the West German state. In 1949, the first Chancellor of the FRG, Konrad Adenauer, proclaimed that "the primary function of the state is to encourage capital formation." As economist Willi Semmler has written: "'state policy was not limited only to Ordungspolitik ('providing a general framework for the market system'), but rather, it intervened massively in favour of the formation of capital."[10]

In pursuit of this aim, the government promoted corporate savings by tax exemptions and generous depreciation allowances. The result was that more than 60 per cent of gross investment came from depreciation and retained profits during the 1950s.[11] Economist Semmler concluded : "The share of consumption in the GNP was very low and decreased from 1950 to 1960 from 64.1 per cent to 56.6 per cent. The share of the state consumption in GNP decreased also from 15.2 per cent in 1950 to 12.8 per cent in 1956 and 13.5 per cent in 1960. At the same time the share of investment in GNP increased from 19.1 per cent in 1950 to 24.2 per cent in 1960. These data make clear that the increases in GNP went neither to private consumption nor to state consumption, but to private investment."[12]

The huge expansion of the West Germany economy would not have been possible without this enormous investment of capital. What was taking place in the space of one decade was the reconstruction of shattered cities, the housing of a population that had been increased by ten million refugees and the rebuilding and upgrading of the country's industrial plant. All this required capital investment, and although German savings grew from roughly 3 per cent to 9 per cent of GDP during the decade,[13] savings alone were far from sufficient to finance an expansion.

The hero of West German economic takeoff during the 1950s was Ludwig Erhart, finance minister in the Christian Democrat (CDU) government, the prime architect of the "social market economy," a market system that was also to guarantee social security as its name implied. For American observers it was the success of the market system that registered, but, in fact, West Germany's high rate of growth was due to a market system in which a large role was played by the state.

Aftermath of the Miracle

In the 1960s the West German economy continued to grow, but less rapidly, with the country falling behind France and Italy in the pace of expansion. (While German real GDP growth averaged 4.1 per cent a year from 1960 to 1968, French growth averaged 5.4 per cent and that of Italy 5.7 per cent.)[14] An important reason for slower growth was that the country experienced labour shortage problems, brought on, in part, by the building in 1961 of the Berlin Wall, which stopped the flow of migrants from East Germany. While from 1951 to 1960 the labour force grew from 20.9 million workers to 26 million workers, during the following decade there was only a tiny expansion to 26.2 million workers.[15] As a result West Germany rapidly increased its use of foreign workers from 250,000 in 1960 to 1.8 million by 1970 — by the latter date they constituted nearly 7 per cent of the labour force.[16] The end of the large-scale influx of skilled German workers from the east meant that future economic expansion would depend above all on increased productivity, which was pursued by West German industry through massive investment in capital equipment.

The economy continued to be heavily dependent on exports with 33.4 per cent of vehicles sold abroad, along with 29.2 per cent of machinery.[17] The crucial role of exports can be seen in the economic cycles of the sixties, in which an upturn in exports led soon to general recovery in the form of increased investments and increased domestic demand. With ups and downs reflecting the economic cycle, capital investment remained strong through the decade, in several years exceeding 25 per cent of GDP.

By the mid-1960s, the political environment in West Germany had become much more complex than it had been in the previous decade. The Christian Democrats (CDU) had been continually in power from the time of the founding of the FRG. The battle of economic survival had been won, in stunning fashion, and with victory the consensus which had previously existed began to erode. Up until then the West German government had stuck to its emphasis on capital accumulation and investment at the expense of wages and salaries, and had not made any effort to pursue a counter- cyclical (Keynesian) fiscal policy. By the mid-1960s German workers were becoming highly critical of a policy which appeared to be at their expense. They had played a major part in rebuilding the economy and they wanted their reward.

In 1966, the CDU lost considerable support in national elections and the result was a new coalition government in which the CDU shared power with their traditional major opponents, the Social Democrats (SPD), led by Willi Brandt. In the next election in 1969, the SPD came to power in coalition with the small centrist party, the Free Democrats (FDP). With the Social Democrats in office first under Willi Brandt and later under Helmut Schmidt, government policy became officially Keynesian, with Bonn pledged to use fiscal policy to moderate economic cycles. Keynesianism, however, was not to be an unalloyed success. For one thing, the West German state was much more decentralized than pre- war Germany had been. Under its federal system, the lander (states) had significant power to carry out their own policies and to raise their own tax revenues, thereby making a centrally coordinated fiscal policy difficult to achieve with any precision. Moreover, Keynesian counter-cyclical policies were soon to confront the same difficulties in West Germany that they faced elsewhere in the problematic economic environment of the 1970s, with its twin ills of slow growth and high inflation.

If West Germany's fiscal policy was to prove problematic for the domestic economy, Bonn's monetary policy was to produce problems for the entire international monetary system. It was the consistent aim of the West German government and central bank to hold down the value of the Deutschmark (DM) against other currencies. A low Deutschmark assisted the country's strong export orientation. If the DM was undervalued, it was easier to sell West German goods abroad and harder for foreigners to sell their products in Germany. In the prevailing system of fixed exchange rates, continual balance of payments surpluses meant that West Germany acquired huge reserves of foreign currency. Although West Germany was forced under the circumstances to give in to moderate upward revaluations of the DM, the currency remained seriously undervalued, very much in line with the desires of the Bonn government. This policy exerted serious strains on the Bretton Woods agreement of fixed exchange rates and, in the circumstances of the early 1970s, it became an important factor in the overturning of the system and its replacement with floating exchange rates.

During the 1970s, the country's real GDP grew less quickly than that of all the other major industrial nations except Britain. Following the OPEC oil price revolution of 1973, German growth in GDP fell sharply, to an average of 2.3 per cent a year until 1979, lower than that of Japan, France, Italy, Canada and the United States.[18] These aggregate real GDP figures, however, tend to exaggerate how poorly West Germany was faring in relation to other countries. Part of the reason for the slowing of general growth had to do with the fact that the country's population actually declined between 1975 and 1980 (from 61.8 million to 61.4 million) and the size of the German labour force during this period increased only slightly (from 26.884 million to 27.217 million).[19] In all the other major industrialized countries, the labour force grew by widely varying but significant amounts during the same years.

By other measures, which control for population, the West German economic performance was stronger. For the period 1973 to 1979, Germany's real GDP per capita was second among the seven major industrialized countries, at 2.5 per cent per year, with only France ahead at 2.6 per cent.[20] Also for the same period, in growth in real GDP per person employed, Germany was first among the seven, tied with Japan, at 2.9 per cent per year.[21]

The social peace that had resulted from the post-war consensus about the direction of the society and economy came under further pressure in the seventies. By German standards, there was a large increase in the number of strikes, although their occurrence was still rare compared to other countries. In 1972, the SPD government enacted a new Works Constitution Act which further extended the concept of worker representation in company decision-making. Four years later, co-determination of industry was again extended to embrace all joint stock companies in the country with more than 2000 employees. Because it meant that workers' representatives had an effective means of influencing company policy and of finding out for themselves just what constraints confronted industry, the system led to fewer confrontations. It gave workers and their representatives a greater stake in the well-being of enterprises than their counterparts in countries with a more adversarial labour-management tradition, such as Britain, the United States and Canada. The changes enacted in the 1970s gave worker representatives rights of two kinds: works council rights, in matters of social welfare and personnel policy; and co-determination rights (in most large firms) in deciding matters of business policy.

By the 1980s, it was clear that the West German formula for economic success was badly in need of being reformulated. Although the country did not fare as badly as the United States and Canada in the severe recession of 1981-82, its recovery took longer, and once underway it was so slow that the expansion of all Western Europe was held back. While real GDP declined in the United States in 1982 by 3 per cent, and in Canada by 4.3 per cent, in Germany the decline was a much more moderate .6 per cent.[22] However, unemployment in West Germany climbed from 3.3 per cent in 1980 to 8.2 per cent in 1983 and in the spring of 1987 it was 8.7 per cent.[23] Despite the slowness of recovery, West German policy was extremely cautious. In part, the caution stemmed from the historic fear Germans have of inflation, a fear dating to the 1920s. It also stemmed from the return to power of the Christian Democrats in 1982, under Helmut Kohl. With the right replacing the left in power, there was no possibility of a German repeat of Francois Mitterand's experiment in France, an attempt on the part of the French government to reflate its national economy in defiance of the global recession. Instead, the German government preached restraint and the cutting back of the public sector deficit, arguing that economic growth would resume when conditions for investment had been restored by rebuilding confidence through the reduction of the public debt.[24]

Rather than undertake measures to increase German domestic economic demand, the government relied on huge new opportunities for exports to the United States and on declining world oil prices to promote recovery. Germany's very strong export performance was again the central feature of expansion. Indeed by 1986, German trade surpluses along with those of Japan, when coupled with the huge deficits of the United States, had created a crisis in the global economy.

Intervention in West Germany

As we have seen, the state has played a key role in the economic development of West Germany. The Bonn government took a crucial part in designing an economy in which rapid capital accumulation, industrial exports, an undervalued Deutschmark and industrial co-determination were hallmarks. Ironically, intervention in launching the West German economy came from Washington as well as from Bonn. The Marshall Plan, the encouragement of German re- industrialization during the Korean War and the vast military spending of the U.S. abroad — much of it in West Germany — were crucial to the making of the "miracle." Taken as a whole, the international economic system over which America presided, with its export of American capital through multinationals and defence spending, and its perennial U.S. current-account deficit, helped create an environment in which the export-led West German economy could thrive.

Intervention has also taken the form of a battery of measures which have served as the mechanisms for West German industrial strategy. As do many industrial countries, West Germany deploys tax concessions and subsidies as "defensive" measures to shore-up existing industries, in addition to research and development support for industries where potential technological and market breakthroughs can be made.[25] Tax concessions have been concentrated in transportation, housing and construction as well as in the promotion of industry in particular regions. Subsidies have been aimed mainly at energy, mining and agriculture, with increasing emphasis on the upgrading of industrial technology. In 1985, these programs cost 36.35 billion DM.[26] West Germany also provides direct, large-scale support for technologically innovative sectors. In recent years this effort has been strengthened as the country struggles to maintain technological parity with Japan and the United States. Bonn has provided funding to defray research and development manpower costs for innovative firms involved in the development of new products and processes. Under this program, it also allows rapid depreciation of the capital invested in R and D. Two very large projects have formed the centre of this public-sector effort: the development of a large mainframe Siemens computer; and the designing of new aircraft at Airbus, the western

European aircraft consortium.[27] Both of these efforts have been controversial. The issue in both cases is whether public funding can ever make these projects fully successful, one day able to stand on their own without further infusions of public investment.

Micro-electronics and aerospace are the big leagues of today's high technology, forbidding territory even for so formidable an economic power as West Germany. In the case of micro-electronics, Germany and all of Western Europe have been watching the battle for supremacy between the Japanese and the Americans, feeling themselves at times to be little more than bystanders. The Germans have concluded that to be a first rank economic power, they cannot be completely dependent on Japan and the United States for access to advanced micro-electronic technology.

Airbus Industrie Inc. — the focus of West Germany's aerospace effort — is a consortium in which West Germany (37.9 per cent), France (37.9 per cent), Britain (20 per cent), and Spain (4.2 per cent) are partners. The European company announced plans in 1986 to develop two long-range aircraft: the A-330, a twin-engined, 310-passenger aircraft with a range of 5,800 miles; and the A-340, a 260 plus passenger jet with four engines and a range of up to 7,800 miles. The two aircraft, to be built by the early 1990s, will come as a package, sharing 80 per cent of their components, thus making them each much cheaper. If successful, the two aircraft will compete with the Boeing 767 and the longer-range Boeing 747. (In January 1987, the German airliner Lufthansa, 75 per cent owned by the Bonn government, placed the first firm order for the new aircraft.)[28] To date, eight billion dollars in western European public revenues has been invested in Airbus. As in the case of West Germany's micro-electronic efforts, the controversy surrounding Airbus concerns long-run viability. Will the new aircraft end up as technical marvels and commercial white elephants such as the Anglo-French Concorde, or will their development lead to a successful penetration of the global aircraft market?

There is no easy way, at present, to assess the effectiveness of West Germany's efforts to stay abreast of high technology. The specific projects that are being funded today will take years to bear fruit or to be proven as dead ends. The deployment of robots in the industrial process is one such project. In 1986, the OECD issued a productivity study which compared the extent to which various countries use industrial robots. In 1983, West Germany made use of 4,800 industrial robots, compared with 8,000 in the United States and 16,500 in Japan.

More significant, for each 10,000 workers employed in manufacturing, Germany deployed 4.6 industrial robots, ahead of the United States at 4.0, but well behind Japan at 13.0 and Sweden at 29.9.[29] In terms of the general growth of labour productivity in manufacturing, the same study concluded that, for the period 1975 to 1981, West Germany outperformed the United States, Britain and Canada, while being behind Italy, France and Japan.[30]

Two other areas of West German industrial policy are domestic procurement practices and state ownership of industry.

While it is not possible to put a figure on the extent to which West German state agencies practice the deliberate purchase of domestic over foreign products to bolster these industries, it is clear that domestic preference is a factor in such purchases. Two industries where this has been true are computers and coal. A study of the purchasing of large mainframe computers by the German public sector revealed a strong tendency to favour Telefunken and Siemens, the domestic producers, over IBM.[31] While the coal industry is hardly an example of high technology, there has been a combination of practices — tariffs, subsidies and administrative persuasion — to promote the sale of domestic over foreign coal.[32] Here domestic procurement has been favoured both to ease the country's overwhelming dependence on imported fuels and also to maintain the employment of workers in the Ruhr area.

State ownership of industry does not have as high a profile in West Germany as it does in other western countries, most notably in France. Nevertheless, the state's investment in industry is considerable. Generally speaking, state holdings are dispersed in a wide number of sectors, and the state-owned or partly state-owned companies, are not run by a centralized government super-agency. The two highest profile companies which are partly government-owned are Veba, the Chemical and energy giant, which is 40 per cent owned by the federal government, and Volkswagen, which is 16 per cent owned by the federal government and 20 per cent by the State of Lower Saxony.[33]

The state-owned sector, while not operated through a centrally operated agency, nonetheless gives the German government greater leverage in carrying out its economic policies.

American businessmen have long admired German hard work, discipline, reliability and entrepreneurship, often producing homilies on how these are the keys to success. When they think fondly of another economy, there is no doubt that their thoughts turn most often to West Germany. It is fair to conclude, however, that their admiration has been for only half of the equation — the market half, and that they have failed to understand West German interventionism.

Part of this lack of understanding stems from looking at what the Germans say rather than at what they do. Formally, the West Germans avoid state planning. For them there never was a "planning vogue" of the kind that existed in France. German interventionism rather has taken the form of a series of industrial policies combined with a meshing of the state and private sectors. The aim has been to strive for consensus in German society around major goals.

Rhetorically, the West German government of Helmut Kohl has in recent years offered a program that bears a strong resemblance to the conservative programs being promulgated elsewhere in the capitalist world: privatization, deregulation, reduction of subsidies to industries. In practice, however, there have been very few steps toward privatization, in marked contrast to Margaret Thatcher's Britain, and the average level of subsidization of industry has not declined at all.

Still, if interventionism remains as strong as ever, there is today little evidence of the large imagination and creativity that launched the takeoff of the West German economy in the fifties. The country has stuck doggedly to the formula that made it great over three decades ago — strong exports combined with low inflation and a sound currency. This combination was extremely effective in an era when the United States was economically supreme. At the end of the 1980s, however, the situation is radically altered; the great American import engine is no longer strong enough to carry the global economy. Having supplied 70 per cent of the increased demand in the capitalist world in the first years of the recovery from the 1981-82 recession, the United States is now drowning in a sea of red ink. The West German formula has now been pushed past the point of no return. Even with the huge trade surpluses of the mid-1980s — in excess of $50 billion in 1986 — West German unemployment has remained stuck at about 8.5 per cent, a far cry from the 1 per cent unemployment of the late 1950s.

West Germany now needs to embark on a new economic course that will require as much boldness as the takeoff in the 1950s did. Such a strategy can only be conceived in terms of Western Europe as a whole, a daunting prospect when one considers just how difficult European economic coordination has been. Without such a new strategy, however, West Germany will waver between success and failure, a trim exporting machine, but a country unable to provide anything like full employment for its people.

Chapter Six

France: Battleground of Economic Ideas

Four French jet fighters sweep in tight formation over the dry, hilly landscape of Provence. Frequent sonic booms rattle the windows of the ancient farm houses below, annoying the farmers who go about their work with little modern machinery. The scene captures the dual nature of the contemporary French economy. There is a modern France, complete with high tech competitive industry and an old-fashioned France with a fractured, localized inefficient economy.

The two Frances are cheek by jowl in a country which has been undergoing a fundamental debate on economic strategy during the 1980s. France faces the very real problem of being number two in Western Europe, still well behind West Germany, whose economy has been growing rapidly and sucking in investment from the rest of the continent. France is well aware that technological independence does not come cheap in the late twentieth century. While the French have West German success to tempt and frustrate them, they also have the negative model of British de-industrialization to warn them of the price of failure. In addition, France has been spurred on by the continuing problem of high unemployment — over two million were jobless in 1986, and of this number 700,000 had been without work for more than a year.[1]

French politics in the 1980s has been marked by contrast, by a genuine conflict of ideas about the key issue for a contemporary economy — how to modernize. Twice during the decade, the people of France have chosen options of principle to solve their problems —

turning to the left in 1981 and to the right in 1986. In both cases, they have become quickly disillusioned with the ability of first the left and then the right to deliver on their visions for the country.

Starting Afresh

Before we can make sense of the great debate of the eighties, we need to look at the development of France's economy in the post-war period. France emerged from the Second World War as a nation that had been shaken to its roots. It had been on the winning side, but had suffered considerable economic losses — the railways and industries in northern France were devastated. At the psychological level, moreover, France, in a very real sense, had been a loser in the conflict. The catastrophic defeat of the French military in the spring of 1940 by the Nazi blitzkrieg has haunted France ever since. No less damaging to the national spirit was internal division during the war. The unspeakable fact was that collaboration with the Germans was much more widespread than the French after the war would like to think, while the Resistance was much smaller, especially in the first three years of the occupation, than national pride would like to concede. France emerged from the conflict haunted by its past weakness and its half- buried internal conflicts.

In 1945 France, gravely divided politically, entered a period in which the lifetime of governments was very short. And yet, during this period of political uncertainty, so characteristic of the Fourth Republic, the country experienced rapid economic growth, spurred by the leadership of the public sector. During the 1950s, France's industrial production grew by 44 per cent, compared with 26 per cent in Britain.[2] The apparent paradox of the Fourth Republic is resolved by the fact that while governments in France were weak, the state was strong.

The American Marshall Plan and the general renewal of growth throughout the western world were important factors in France's economic revival, but there was much more to it than that. For centuries, France had had a tradition of strong state leadership in national life, going back to Louis XIV, to Colbert, to Napoleon. In an hour of national crisis and threatened national disintegration, it was natural that the country would turn to its statist tradition. In this case the state was to be the instrument for economic renewal. In undertaking the task of national reconstruction, there was continuity with the strong state role of the past. But there was discontinuity in the assumption that the national economy could be made to grow steadily.

The war had discredited many of the older bureaucrats who normally would have been in a position of leadership in the French public service. Instead a new corps of well trained, highly motivated technocrats became the central force in initiating and implementing planned economic renewal. Under the leadership of Jean Monnet in 1946, the Commissariat- General du Plan — the state agency that was to oversee the "Plan" — was established.[3] The new technocrats were young men of intense zeal, products of the elitist system of French education, graduates of the Grandes Écoles. They shared an outlook in common, a belief in the potential to transform the French economy, that gave them the character of shock troops in a national struggle.

The five-year First Plan was approved in 1946, with Jean Monnet as the Commissioner-General of its Secretariat. The Plan was intended to establish guidelines for the future course of the economy, to set priorities, and to point out ways for government and the private sector to overcome problems and achieve goals. With a full-time small secretariat of never more than forty individuals, the Plan sought the cooperation of both government and industry to pursue the guidelines it established. In the early years, the Plan was immensely successful in winning support from both public and private sectors and in encouraging the players in the national economy to work together to achieve common goals. It set goals for specific industries, as well as for the general growth of the economy. Once these goals had been broadly outlined, they were submitted to twenty-five "modernization commissions" whose job it was to work out in detail how progress could be achieved in specific sectors. These "modernization commissions" were the real heart of the Plan and they marked a clear break with the French tradition of formal bureaucracy. In the "modernization commissions," planners, entrepreneurs from large and small companies, and union representatives met intensively for months to thrash out a scheme for achieving success. There was more than a little resemblance between this process and the "consensus forums" operated by the Ministry of International Trade and Industry (MITI) in Japan.

The Plan's modernization commissions helped to create a common approach to the problems of a particular sector that pushed the major players in the industry together. Two analysts writing about the collaborative aspects of the Plan stated that "the main originality of French planning, compared with systems tried elsewhere, is that the preparation of the Plan also involves 'concertation.' This means that the main interest groups present, debate, argue and confront their different objectives and points of view."[4] There was no coercive state intervention here, no command economy. French planning was voluntary and indicative, leaving the private sector very much alive. But the result was quite different from what was achieved in the enterprise economic model. Private sector companies, having had crucial input into the Plan, ended up thinking of it as theirs, which indeed it was.

The Plan thus gave cohesion to national economic effort. It not only set priorities for the major players in the economy, it pointed to ways the government could assist specific industries through tax breaks, subsidies or other measures. The first Plan (1946-52) took the long view in choosing the reconstruction of basic industries such as coal, steel and electricity as the highest priority. The second Plan (1953-7) broadened the emphasis to foster the general growth of industry and agriculture. The third (1958-61) and fourth (1962-5) Plans included the meeting of social goals in welfare and housing and increased the priority of regional development. In the 1970s and 1980s, the Plans were to employ advanced econometric models of the economy to assist in their forecasting.[5]

Originally, the Plan had the great advantage of being perceived as non-political, as not attached to the fleeting fortunes of the ever-changing ministries of the Fourth Republic. By the 1970s and 1980s, however, both the left and the right in France found the Plan objectionable in significant ways. The left came to see the Plan as a product of technocratic elitism handed down from on high, as contributing to France's already too-centralized character. The right saw it as the work of left-wing civil servants, as interfering with the functioning of the market system. Trade unionists also grew suspicious that they were being co-opted in the seductive atmosphere of the "modernization commissions," and from an early date the Communist-led CGT (Confédération générale du travail) withdrew from their proceedings.

In the past two decades the Plan has lost importance for several reasons: the increasing integration of the French economy into that of western Europe; the diffusion of the techniques of the Plan's secretariat to other departments of government; and the emergence of a sharp ideological debate between left and right about the French economy. France's integration into the economy of western Europe proceeded rapidly after the Treaty of Rome of 1957 established the common market. As France's exports to and imports from common market countries increased dramatically, planning for France itself became intrinsically more problematic, although by no means impossible. To a considerable extent, the second factor, the spreading of planning techniques throughout the French government was an outcome of the success of the Plan, but it nonetheless had the effect of duplicating or making redundant much of the work carried out by the secretariat. With regard to the third factor, as long as Charles de Gaulle remained in power the notion of planning was not the preserve of either the left or the right in French politics. That was to change in the 1970s, however. Under the Presidency of Valery Giscard D'Estaing, the right was to shift toward "liberalism," the economics of the market place and away from the notion of economic planning. At the same time, the left was to demand nationalization of the key sectors of the economy as the core of its program. As France moved out of the era of post-war rebuilding and as fairly rapid economic growth came to be seen as normal, the consensus on which planning had been based was disintegrating.

Disillusionment with the Plan also stemmed from the pattern of France's economic performance. Before 1973, France achieved an enviable record of economic growth. While in the 1950s West German growth had outpaced France, after 1960 French growth was significantly higher than that of West Germany, as well as being higher than that of the United States and Britain. Real Gross Domestic Product (GDP) grew in France by 5.4 per cent per year from 1960 to 1968, compared with 4.5 per cent in the U.S., 4.1 per cent in West Germany and 3.1 per cent in Britain; from 1968 to 1973, French GDP increased by an average of 5.9 per cent per year, ahead of West Germany at 4.9 per cent and well ahead of the United States at 3.3 per cent and Britain at 3.2 per cent. Only Japan stayed well ahead of France during this period.[6] In terms of productivity advance, France's achievement was also noteworthy. From 1965 to 1973, France's productivity growth in the manufacturing sector was 6.7 per cent per year, behind Japan's stunning 11 per cent but well ahead of the United States at 2.5 per cent.[7]

After the first oil price shock in 1973, French economic advance, like that in the rest of the industrialized world, slowed appreciably before picking up again, although not to pre-1973 levels. Between 1973 and 1979, France's real GDP grew by 3.1 per cent per year, putting it again well ahead of growth in the United States, West Germany and Britain.[8] French productivity growth in manufacturing slowed to 1.5 per cent a year from 1973 to 1975 and then advanced to 3.9 per cent from 1975 to 1981.[9] Slower growth in France after 1973 was reflected in a dramatic surge in unemployment from 2.6 per cent in 1973 to 7.3 per cent in 1981.[10]

Valery Giscard D'Estaing, elected president of France in 1974, was seen as the supreme embodiment of French technocracy, himself a graduate of both the École Polytechnique and the École Nationale d'-Adminstration, the major recruiting ground for top administrators. While he was committed to a shift toward a more market-directed economy, he surrounded himself with a team of technocrats which became increasingly unpopular in the era of slower growth and higher unemployment at the end of the 1970s and beginning of the 1980s. Unemployment, which had been 2.8 per cent when Giscard took power in 1974, reached 7.3 per cent by the time he was defeated in 1981.[11]

Changing economic fortunes contributed to the tide of dissatisfaction that swept Francois Mitterand to power in the presidential elections of 1981, a victory that was followed by a Socialist win in the subsequent national assembly elections. The French Socialists were committed to a classical social democratic programme which included:

- widespread nationalization of industry, to put the key levers of economic development in the public sector.

- the elaboration of a *dirigiste* industrial strategy, so that government authorities could plan the future direction of industry, an exercise which would both revive and make more potent the notion of planning in France. (This differed from the Plan in two respects: it was intended that planning would operate in the context of a much expanded public sector; and it was intended that planning would be more decentralized and democratic than in the past.)

- the pumping of very large sums of money into traditional industries to guarantee their survival and to ensure the creation of new jobs.

- the spending of public money on social programs and public works to reflate the economy, as a strategy for reducing unemployment.

- democratization of industry.

The French left was determined to change the very shape of French society, to make France a beacon in the development of human liberation and socialism. During the election campaign, Mitterand had presented the electorate with the so-called 110 propositions — a program of transformation whose purpose was to make France the citadel for the "liberation of man and the construction of socialism." The Socialists aimed for political liberalization, decentralization and workers' rights — no less than a "new style of citizenship."[12] The problem was that the lofty goals were not matched by a realistic appreciation of just how difficult it would be to change the direction of the French economy, given two circumstances: France's integration into the international economic system, and the hostility of the powerful French private sector to the goals. Moreover, the new government's timing could not have been worse, since it set out on its course of reform just as the deep recession of 1981-82 gripped the global economy.

But the Socialists had faith that the levers of state power would overcome whatever barriers stood in their way. Boldly, they embarked on a program of spending that was designed to boost demand and thereby to create jobs. The strategy quickly led to a soaring balance of payments deficit. Instead of finding itself on the road to socialism, France was soon heading for international insolvency. What Mitterand's years in power were to show was that the Socialists had a far from perfect understanding of how the economy worked and of the limits on a single country's ability to alter conditions prevailing throughout the industrialized world.

Their first big mistake was to think they could virtually ignore the world recession and reflate the French economy through an across-the-board increase in public-sector spending and workers' wages. Here they were employing traditional social democratic medicine, a classical Keynesian macro-economic policy. What happened was that France enjoyed a brief boom all of its own. Then came disaster.

The French people — just as they were supposed to — spent more money, thereby increasing domestic demand. But French imports soared, while exports stagnated. The country's trade deficit worsened dramatically, from 20 billion francs in 1980 to 105 billion in 1981. Increased government spending brought a huge increase in the public-sector deficit, which quadrupled between 1980 and 1983. The immediate result of the strategy was an increase in inflation to 14 per cent in 1981 and then successive devaluations of the Franc.[13] The lesson was clear: France's integration into the broader international economy was so great that the demand generated at home simply leaked out of the country.

By the spring of 1982, the Socialists recognized that their treatment was causing France's economy to hemorrhage. They did a policy U-Turn. Public spending was sharply curtailed under austerity programs adopted in 1982 and the spring of 1983. Temporary wage and price controls were imposed. These policies succeeded in getting France's balance of payments problem under control and salvaged the franc from further devaluation. Inflation also began a slow decline from 13.4 per cent in 1981, to 11.8 per cent in 1982, and then 9.6 per cent and 7.4 per cent in 1983 and 1984.[14]

Lesson one had been learned. Unfortunately for the Socialists, they made one other big mistake and it had to do with industrial strategy. They began with the romantic notion that if you threw enough money at the traditional industries you could make them viable. Any industry could be made competitive if it was nationalized and given a proper capital base, the theory went. The Socialist government pumped tens-of-billions of francs into taking over banks and industries and rebuilding the capital base of companies already in the public sector. In 1981-82 they spent forty-seven billion francs to acquire twelve industrial firms (including seven of the country's largest twenty), thirty-six banks and two finance companies.[15]

The newly nationalized companies were added to an already large public sector, whose companies were on average more productive and competitive than those in the private sector (with 18 per cent of the work-force, they accounted for 25 per cent of value added).

To understand the context in which the new nationalizations were occurring, we need to briefly examine the nationalizations of the past. The two periods in which nationalizations had been most widespread were 1936, when the Popular Front government had been in power; and 1944 to 1946, just after the Liberation, when the move against private companies was associated with the belief that French capitalists had often been Nazi collaborators. The Popular Front had taken over armaments companies, the railways and had partially nationalized the Bank of France. The post-war government went much further, taking over Renault, the auto company, Air France, coal, electrical and gas companies, major insurance companies and the rest of the Bank of France.[16]

But conservative regimes had added their own share of large- scale nationalization as well. In the thirteen years before 1981, when the Socialists came to power, the workforce of the publicly owned industrial sector had been increased by more than 300,000. By 1981, over 20 per cent of the value added, and 60 per cent of industrial research, was centred in the nationalized industries. In addition, three-quarters of bank deposits were in the hands of the state through a variety of public and semi-public institutions, which gave the government a very tight control over the allocation of capital in France. Thus "backdoor" nationalization had already created a very large public sector before the Socialists came to power with a program designed to extend this still further.

During and following the recession, horror stories of losses in the public sector abounded. In one year, Renault, the publicly-owned automaker lost more money than any company in the nation's history — ten billion francs in 1984.[17] Iron and steel lost seven billion francs in 1981 and again in 1982 and ten billion francs in 1983. Total losses among publicly-owned industrial companies reached eleven billion francs in 1981, nineteen billion in 1982 and seventeen billion in 1983.[18]

One problem with the government's approach was that it was far too indiscriminate in spreading its largesse through the public sector — it acted as though its means were unlimited. But there was another reason for the failure of the Socialist government's policies. In an era of very rapid technological change, France needed specialization, needed to pick niches for success in international markets. To some degree the Socialist government understood the problem, and this was reflected in the constant talk of "modernization." However, rhetoric and action did not coincide. The government poured enormous amounts of money into traditional sectors — steel, coal and agriculture, which necessarily took away from the amount that could be invested in more promising areas. Of course, there were obvious reasons why the government pumped money into these industries. If the strategy worked, it would create jobs in the blue collar working class, a key constituency of support for the Socialist Party.

As was the case with macro-economic policy, the Socialists learned their lesson in the field of industrial strategy. Unfortunately, the two errors had been mutually reinforcing. Having nearly bankrupted the country with their broad spending policy, they soon had very little money left to make investments in industry, even in industrial sectors which had real promise. By 1982 there was a new realism in government policies. Painful decisions to streamline traditional industries were taken. Steel and coal plants were shut down and thousands of workers lost their jobs in regions such as Lorraine, leading to working class disillusionment with the government. The Socialists discovered the importance of the "firm" to economic well-being. Entrepreneurs, previously disdained, were now seen as key to France's economic salvation. Technological change and modernization rather than job creation became the main aim of industrial policy.

Having lowered their sights from changing society to managing the economy, the Socialists proved themselves able to guide industry toward winnable goals and new international competitiveness. The successes of the French economy are there to be seen. One of them is the vaunted TGV, the fastest passenger train in the world. Riding this train at 270 kilometers an hour one summer day, I was astonished to find myself two-thirds of the way from Paris to Geneva in an hour. France and other European partners share the success of Airbus, the western European aircraft consortium which is now ready to take on the giant American firms. Moreover, French productivity increases, although growing more slowly than in the past, continued well ahead of those in the United States between 1981 and 1984.

Yet one intractable problem remained — unemployment. Instead of holding down unemployment as the government had hoped, France's jobless rate went on climbing from 8.1 per cent in 1982 to 8.3 per cent the following year, to 9.7 per cent in 1984.[19]

In the end, bad luck — the coincidence of power with the severe recession of 1981-82 — and bad management — the mistakes of the first year or two in power — cost the Socialists control of the National Assembly in the elections of March 1986. Despite their costly mistakes, however, the French Socialists succeeded in making themselves a viable alternative governing party during the 1980s. They learned how to pursue the goal of industrial rebuilding, without heading the nation toward a balance of payments crisis. They moved French socialism away from the traditional "big spender" policies that have been the common legacy of international social democracy toward the more fertile ground of workable industrial strategy.

The Right in Power

The National Assembly elections of March 1986 brought a coalition of right-wing parties to power with Jacques Chirac as Prime Minister. Chirac, leader of the party that is the successor to the Gaullist formation in French politics, espoused a program called "liberalism," a program that in the English-speaking world would be described as "neo-conservative." Chirac's program involved rolling back state power in France, reversing many of the nationalizations undertaken by the Socialists during their years in power and strengthening the private sector in the economy. To British and American observers, it would be easy to think of Chirac as a French version of Margaret Thatcher or Ronald Reagan since he stands for the limiting of state power and for placing limits on the extent of the welfare state. The difference is one of context, and it is crucial. Jacques Chirac is prime minister of a country where state power is much more extensive than in any English-speaking country. Moreover, the power of the state in France, as we have seen, has been at least as much a product of the right as it has of the left. Chirac's political ideas and program need to be understood from this perspective, otherwise they will be misinterpreted.

A more fruitful comparison for Chirac than Thatcher and Reagan is Helmut Kohl, the cautious West German Chancellor, a man who is also committed in principle to rolling back the power of the state but who rarely does much about it. The new Chirac government did not take long after its electoral victory to pass a law enabling it to de-nationalize sixty- five publicly-owned companies. Over the next year, however, the government proceeded very slowly with its privatization program, offering a few major companies for sale on the market and taking the symbolically important step of privatizing the country's oldest television channel, TF1. But after fifteen months in power, it was not unreasonable to conclude that the Chirac government was much more cautious about curtailing the state than the Socialists had been about extending it. France retained a very large public sector, which continued to form the centre of many of its major industries.

It should be noted, of course, that the right-wing government in France has not had anything like full power. Francois Mitterand retains the Presidency and has remained very popular with the electorate, while Chirac has suffered as a result of his performance during a series of crises — a spate of terrorist bombings, a hugely successful student strike which forced the government to withdraw a law for the reform of universities, rotating public sector strikes and a strike that disrupted railways and public transit. As long as "cohabitation" continues — the French term for the sharing of power between a Socialist President and a right-wing Prime Minister — French politics will remain in an embroiled transitional state which will not be resolved until the Presidential elections are held in 1988.

The economy's performance has also not helped the right since its return to power. While economic growth overall has stayed at just over 2 per cent a year, unemployment climbed to 11.1 per cent by April 1987.[20] France's economic growth has remained stuck at a level where the severe problem of youth unemployment cannot be addressed. Moreover, the country's room to manoeuvre in reflating its economy has been severely limited by West Germany's refusal to take any steps to increase domestic demand in its own economy. The difficulty is that, as the largest economy in the European Community, West Germany tends to set the pace for its neighbours. With the West German inflation rate running at an annual rate of -0.2 per cent in the spring of 1987, while France's inflation was 3.4 per cent, the French government feared that any attempt to increase internal economic demand to create jobs would lead to increased imports from countries such as West Germany whose industries remained cost-competitive despite upward revaluations of the Deutschmark.

Neo-conservatism has had hard going with public opinion since the right came to power. A report by the SOFRES polling organization showed only 26 per cent of people had a positive impression of the Chirac government's first hundred days in power, while 48 per cent had a negative impression. Polls such as this are no different from the ones that earlier indicated dissatisfaction with the Socialists when they were in power, but they suggest that the French people are not in the mood for a sharp shift in the direction that right-wing ideologues might hope to take.

Instead of doing what either the right or the left would truly like, French people seem to want to stay with the mixed economy approach which has worked well most of the time during the period since the war. Public opinion polls indicate support for the idea of privatization in the abstract along with resistance to it whenever it is actually suggested in a concrete case. While this ambivalence has annoyed politicians, it reflects a strong current of support for staying the course that France has actually been on.

For people in English-speaking countries, who are used to thinking of France as a land of intrusive bureaucracy, this insistence on staying with the strong role of the state has been something of a mystery. What is hard for outsiders to grasp is that the French state has played a key role in making France's economy the success it has been. To push and prod French industry toward success, the interventionist French state has provided tax breaks, favourable loans, guaranteed access to needed credit and government markets for domestic products. And while neo-conservatives regard such intervention as anathema, the fact is that, for the past twenty years, French industry has regularly outperformed its North American counterpart in terms of productivity increases. Since the mid-1960s, French annual increases in productivity have been about twice those achieved in Canada and the United States. The result is that France has come close to eliminating the productivity gap between its industry and North American industry.

Moreover, the state plays a large role not only in the ownership and guiding of industry, but also in support for a highly advanced welfare state. France spends a higher proportion of its GDP — 26.0 per cent in 1983 — on outlays for its system of social programs than any other major industrialized country. This compares with Italy (19.4 per cent), West Germany (17.1 per cent), Britain (13.7 per cent), Canada (12.5 per cent), the United States (12.1 per cent) and Japan (11.3 per cent).[21] The system provides:

- generous payments to workers whose jobs have been lost because of technological change.

- public payments to cover most medical and dental expenses.

- generous family allowances to those with children.

- rent subsidies for low-income families.

- vacation subsidies for low-income families with children.

- the Maternelles, which extend the public educational system free of charge to children over the age of two-and-a-half. (They attend for four-and-a-half full days a week, if the parents wish to send them.)

- a system of Garderies (day care centres) that provide publicly subsidized service for children under the age of four at a cost to parents of about one dollar an hour.

New measures added while the Socialists were in power include: a shorter, thirty-nine hour work week, without any loss of pay; and five-week paid holidays for most workers.

While neo-conservatives see such programs as examples of state intrusion, they are popular — and not easy to eliminate.

Two conclusions emerge from the protracted French ideological debate of the 1980s. The French private sector is too powerful and too integrated into the broader international economy to be bypassed when it comes to the strategic planning of the economy. On the other hand, the state has played an important role in keeping France competitive in the post-war decades and the French people will not easily tolerate the rolling back of their national state in favour of a theory of greater freedom for enterprise. This has led effectively to deadlock, a barrier to the realizing of the vision of either the left or the right in any remotely pure form. Because France has been blocked at pursuing more rapid economic growth by the policies of its major trading partners, particularly West Germany, it may be that the country will not progress significantly until new initiatives are taken in the context of the whole European Community.

Chapter Seven

Italy: The New Number Five

A generation ago, the British were told that France had passed their country in per capita income and in overall economic size. The information was neither welcome, nor particularly believed, but over the past twenty-five years the British have gradually adjusted to the idea that France really does have the fourth largest industrial, capitalist economy. Now the British have received shocking news again. This time, it is that Italy is passing their country in overall economic weight and it will soon be ahead in per capita income as well.

Indeed the relative size of the British and Italian economies became a lively issue in Italian politics in the winter of 1986-87. The exact size of any economy is hard to measure, and this is true of Italy's to an even greater than usual extent, because of the country's very large "black" economy. A study by the Italian government in the early 1980s turned up more than six million people with second or third jobs — people being taxed only on their first jobs. In all, the study estimated that the black economy made up a minimum of 15.4 per cent of Italy's GDP.

In early 1987, taking into account its black component, Giovanni Goria, Italy's treasury minister, issued a report that his country's GDP had reached $579 billion, ahead of Britain whose GDP was $567 billion.[1] If this estimate was correct, it meant that Italy had replaced Britain as the number five economy in the western world. And, it is not unusual to encounter Italians who are confident that their country will eventually overtake France and become number four. Naturally, this surpassing of Britain, "il sorpasso," as it has been called, was not merely a matter of national pride for Italians; it was the basis for Italy's claim to a greater say in the joint councils of the major industrial powers.

So difficult is it for English-speaking observers to accept Italian economic prowess that it is worth summarizing the facts of the case. During the quarter-century from 1960 to the mid-1980s, Italy, along with France, grew faster than the other major Western European countries, West Germany and Britain. Between 1960 and 1984, Italy's real GDP increased by an average of 3.8 per cent a year, ahead of West Germany (3.1), Britain (2.2) and just behind France (4.0).[2] The consequence of this growth was that Italy significantly narrowed the gap between itself and the first rank industrial powers.

Reconstruction and Renewal

To appreciate the extent of the transformation, we need to understand how far the Italian economy has come since the early post-war period. In 1954, agriculture still accounted for 43 per cent of Italian employment (about the same as in the United States in 1900), with 30 per cent working in industry and 27 per cent in the service sector. By 1980, agricultural employment had diminished to 14 per cent of the total, while industry accounted for 38 per cent and the service sector 48 per cent.[3] Moreover, as Italy advanced from being a semi-agricultural to an industrialized country, its rate of productivity growth was impressive in comparison to the performance in other countries — an average of 3.73 per cent a year from 1950-1983 in Italy against 2.19 per cent in the United States and 2.04 per cent in Britain.[4]

Heavy industry grew prodigiously in Italy in the decades following 1950. While that year Italy produced a mere 129,000 cars and trucks and 2.36 million tons of steel, by 1983 the country turned out 1,565,000 vehicles and 21.68 million tons of steel.[5] In the process of rapid industrialization, Italian society was itself dramatically reordered, since a very large proportion of the new industrial jobs were created in the North and were filled by migrants from the poor, agricultural South. (Throughout the post-war decades, Italy has also experienced a very large emigration of population to other countries.)

Italian economic development has decidedly been of the enterprise-intervention variety, in which both public and private sectors have played key roles. In Italy, to an unusual degree, state intervention has taken the form of direct public ownership of industrial enterprises. Along with a high degree of state ownership, there have been a range of industrial policies, in particular policies aimed at achieving the development of southern Italy. Later, we will examine the character of this state intervention in the Italian economy. First however, we will survey the main aggregate developments in the country's economy from 1950 to the mid-1980s.

Growth in Italy was rapid from 1950 to 1958, and extremely rapid from that date until 1963, after which it slowed. In the period before 1958, expansion was generated both by strong internal demand and by rising exports. Labour costs stayed low, productivity increases were strong, and capital investment during the 1950s was very strong, reaching 24 per cent of GDP in 1958.[6] Since 1958, the European Common Market (created by the Treaty of Rome in 1957) has changed the context of Italian development and promoted the rapid growth of exports and imports, as the country was integrated into the broader economy of Western Europe.

For Italians, the late 1950s and early 1960s have been seen, in retrospect, as a time of economic "miracle." GDP growth was 6.5 per cent a year, capital investment reached a peak of 26 per cent of national income, and the country achieved virtual full employment.[7] Even during these good times, however, Italy was bedevilled by high inflation and a balance of payments deficit. While Italian inflation had been low in the 1950s, in 1963, fuelled by high wage increases, it reached 7.5 per cent, double that in Western Europe as a whole. At the same time, Italian buoyancy fostered a sharp growth in imports. To deal with the resultant balance of payments problem, the Italian government undertook a sharp turn in policy in late 1963 — growth in the money supply was halted and taxes were increased. The effect was to push inflation down to the levels prevailing in the rest of Europe and to return the balance of payments to surplus. But investment and economic growth also fell and have never since reached the rates of the half decade prior to 1963.[8] After a brief pause, growth resumed for the rest of the decade, but a lower rate (it averaged 5.3 per cent a year between 1963 and 1969, still high compared with that in the United States and the rest of Western Europe).[9] The underlying problem in this period was the fall in the investment rate which caused Italian industry to lose the momentum it had achieved in the earlier period.

The mid-1960s shift in Italian economic policies helped boost the country's exports so that 30 per cent of industrial output was exported, including, in some years, over 40 per cent of automobile production. With sales abroad increasing by over 15 per cent a year, Italian growth became much more dependent on exports than it previously had been.

With somewhat slower growth, wages were held down, employment declined and unemployment rose even though large scale emigration was still taking place.

The loss in the share of national income going to labour was a factor, at the end of the 1960s, in growing worker dissatisfaction. Strikes increased, with negative impact on industrial output. While, in the early post-war years, industrial relations had been relatively peaceful, in 1969, nearly thirty-eight million working days were lost due to work stoppages involving seven-and-a-half million workers.[10] Strikes remained an important aspect of the social crises that embroiled Italian society in the 1970s.

The Italian economy resumed a satisfactory rate of growth in the early 1970s, but the first oil price shock hit hard and real GDP declined by 3.6 per cent in 1975, by far the most severe setback experienced in any of the major industrial countries.[11] As well, industrial production plummetted by 9 per cent.[12] From 1972 to 1974, auto production dropped by half-a-million vehicles, more than a quarter of total output.[13] The relative fragility of Italy's industrial economy was indicated by its vulnerability to shocks, in this case a combination of the oil price revolution and the collapse of the post-war international system of fixed exchange rates.

The competitiveness of Italian industry was being attacked from a number of directions simultaneously: work days lost to widespread strikes; the appreciation of the lira against the dollar (fallout from Richard Nixon's new economic policies of 1971); and stagnating industrial investments. To deal with this onset of problems, the Italian government increased public-sector investments in industry, raised outlays for social services and devalued the lira (it lost 25 per cent of its value against the dollar between 1974 and 1979).[14] The results were mixed. Although general growth resumed after the first oil price shock, growth in manufacturing productivity, which had been high compared with other countries before 1973, dropped below gains in Japan, West Germany and France, while staying ahead of the dismal performances in the United States, Britain and Canada.[15]

The most visible sign of the Italian economy's distress after 1973 was higher inflation. For the period to 1979, consumer prices increased an average of 16.1 per cent a year, compared to an average of 9.4 per cent a year in the other major industrialized countries.[16] The second oil price shock in 1979 (after the Iranian revolution) caused a new bout of sharp inflation in Italy, boosting consumer price increases from 14.8

per cent in 1979 to 21.2 per cent in 1980. Only the recession which followed was able to bring Italian inflation down again — to 10.8 per cent in 1984, 8.8 per cent in 1985 and 4.5 per cent in 1986.[17]

But while inflation was wrung out of the economy, the recession was a protracted affair in Italy — in 1981, real GDP grew only 0.2 per cent, followed by -0.5 per cent in 1982 and -0.2 per cent in 1983.[18] Still, the economic decline that resulted from the recession was much less severe than in the United States (-3.0 per cent) and Canada (-4.3 per cent).[19] Recovery came in 1984 when real GDP grew by 2.8 per cent, but growth slowed the next year when GDP expanded by only 2.3 per cent.[20] Moreover, Italian unemployment kept on climbing despite the recovery. From 9.1 per cent in 1982, it increased to 10.6 per cent in 1985.[21]

During and immediately following the recession, a major restructuring took place both in the public and private- sector components of industry. Many Italian companies changed themselves thoroughly to promote their competitiveness — revising managerial procedures, deploying new equipment, inventing and improving products, and searching out niches in foreign markets. By the end of 1986, industrial output was advancing strongly and there was optimism that Italian industry was poised for further gains. The European Commission forecast that Italy would likely grow faster than West Germany, France and Britain in the immediate future.[22]

Before we look at the specifics of Italian industrial strategy, we can round out this survey of the country's development by concluding that Italy has successfully negotiated the transition to a mature industrial economy, albeit one faced with serious structural problems. The gap that had traditionally existed between Italy and the industrial nations of northern Europe has been significantly narrowed. Italian growth in the production of automobiles, chemicals, machinery and steel has made northern Italy one of the great regional success stories in the global economy since the Second World War. One need only compare the region's progress with the industrial decline in the British midlands or the American midwest to underscore the point.

Italian Industrial Policies

On the surface, Italian politics since the Second World War has not appeared to create a context for policy continuity. Governments, as in the French fourth republic, have toppled and been replaced at short intervals. However, Italian politics has been much more stable than frequent changes of government make it appear. Italian politics has rested on a basic deadlock. The Christian Democrats have always been the largest party, with about one-third of the vote. Only slightly less popular has been the Communist Party with about 30 per cent of the vote. Italian politics has turned on keeping the Communists permanently out of office, which has meant that all government coalitions have had to include the Christian Democrats.

This basic stability in political life mirrors the continuity of Italy's economic policies. Since the early post-war period, Italy's economic evolution has involved strong state intervention. The rationale for intervention has been that, because Italy industrialized late in relation to its competitors, an active state-sector was required to help the country catch up. The broad aim has been to overcome economic backwardness — both regional and industrial. The specific major goals have been:

- the promotion of industrial development in southern Italy.

- assistance to small companies.

- development of the heavy industrial sector, in particular of steel, chemicals and aluminum.

- assistance to research and the promotion of advanced technology.

- promotion of Italian exports.[23]

Two methods have been used to achieve these goals: public enterprise; and financial incentives to the private sector. Public ownership of major industrial concerns has been used in Italy to promote rapid development in fields where the country has been weak, and to transform the economy of the South. A crucial example of nationalization, indicative of the purposes of public enterprise, was the takeover of the electric power industry in 1962. The takeover would not have occurred when it did had it not been for the formation of a centre-left government in early 1962 that was dependent in parliament on the support of the Socialist Party. But electric power nationalization was not undertaken merely for ideological reasons. The economic motivation for the policy was to provide the country with a coordinated system of power, particularly for underdeveloped regions. Cheaper power would lower production costs for local industries.[24]

Public enterprises in Italy have characteristically been organized under the management of very large holding companies, the most important of which are the Ente Nazionale Idrocarbieri (ENI), and the Istituto per la Ricostruzione Industriale (IRI). These are the two biggest public enterprises in Western Europe; ENI has an annual turnover of about $27 billion, while IRI's is about $25 billion. ENI is chiefly involved in petroleum and related industries; IRI, with about half-a-million employees, operates firms in a wide range of manufacturing and service activities. IRI subsidiaries include Alitalia, three of the country's five major banks, and major steel and shipbuilding companies.[25]

Taken together, about 15 per cent of the fixed investments in Italian manufacturing are in public enterprises, with particularly heavy concentrations in a number of sectors — iron and steel 49.3 per cent, automobiles 26.6 per cent, and chemicals 21.9 per cent. In 1981, 428,000 manufacturing workers were employed by public enterprises, 13.2 per cent of the total.[26]

As economic development continued, public-sector investment has become increasingly tied to countering regional underdevelopment. Beginning in 1957 the state holding company sector was required to have at least 40 per cent of its total investment in the South (Mezzogiorno), and to place at least 60 per cent of its new investment there. In 1971, this requirement was increased to at least 60 per cent of total investment and a minimum of 80 per cent of new investment.[27] This public-sector investment has been controversial. The establishment of large-scale auto and other industrial plants in the South has undoubtedly created employment there. Whether it has involved the most effective use of capital and whether it has done the best possible job of improving the surrounding regional economy, in terms of infrastructure and the strengthening of local small and medium sized firms, is hotly debated.

Public investment has been one arm of Italian state strategy in the South. The other arm has been state support for private-sector companies operating there. The main forms this support has taken have been as follows:

- In 1957, there was a ten year partial exemption from corporate income tax for plants located in the South and a 50 per cent reduction in another direct tax. (In 1969, this exemption was raised to 70 per cent.)

- Also in 1957, investment grants were created to defray up to 25 per cent of new construction expenses and 10 per cent of the costs of new machinery. In addition, subsidized interest rate loans, to cover up to 65 per cent of investment outlays, were made available to assist small and medium-sized firms (in 1962, all firms, regardless of size, became eligible.)

In the period from 1969-1973 additional measures were taken to give still more weight to the effort to develop the South:

- The national government took over the payment of 25 per cent of contributions owed by private firms for social security, health care and unemployment benefits. (In 1976, this was increased to 100 per cent.)

- A planning process was created to bring government and entrepreneurs together to exchange information on infrastructure improvements to be made by the public sector and the investment intentions of the private sector.

- In 1976, under a new law, the procedure for receiving government grants for projects in the South was greatly simplified.

Between 1969 and 1973, the investment drive in the South by semi-public as well as public entities peaked, reaching 58 per cent of their total investments in the country. After 1974, when Italy was diverted from the drive to develop the South by the impact of the oil price shock, public sector investment shifted to give priority to saving firms from bankruptcy.[28]

The long and varied effort to develop the South has been a partial success. While the share of the total industrial investment located in the South increased substantially from the early 1950s to the late 1970s (from 13 per cent to 22 per cent of the national total), the South's share of manufacturing GDP has increased only slightly from 13 per cent to 14.1 per cent. Per capita GDP in the region increased, after a decline in the fifties, from 65 to 69 per cent of the level of national GDP.[29] Despite the effort at industrialization, agriculture remains the largest sector in the South. And even with migration (2.5 million people moving to the North, and 1.6 million people moving abroad) unemployment has remained well above the national average. In fact, the gap between the national and Southern unemployment rates has actually widened. In 1978, the national rate was 7.2 per cent — that in the South 10.0 per cent.[30] Following the recession of the early 1980s, national unemployment was 10.6 per cent, that in the Mezzogiorno 14.7 per cent — with only 8.7 per cent in the North.[31]

In the abstract one could debate whether the money invested in the South by the public sector was spent as wisely as if the country had simply focused its investments on where it thought it could promote the greatest efficiency. In reality, given the nature of modern Italy, a country politically united only since the late 19th century, and a nation deeply divided socially and culturally between north and south, there was little real alternative to a national effort at putting the country's major regions on a more equal economic footing.

Because an enormous part of Italian industrial strength has been devoted to developing the South, the strategy as a whole has been much more defensive, as opposed to innovative, than it might otherwise have been. However, regional development has not been the only major goal of economic policy. As noted previously, other objectives have been: the support of small firms; the development of heavy industry; the promotion of exports; and the encouragement of research and technological advancement. A central policy element has been the creation of public enterprises to establish new industries to overcome supply bottlenecks in key fields. Prior to 1974, when the oil price shock changed things, public enterprises were used to help bring about sectoral restructuring and technological change.[32] From the time of this crisis to the recovery from the recession in the early 1980s (1974-1982), public enterprises were used in a much more *ad hoc* fashion. In what became a period of crisis management, the highest priority was preserving jobs, and to this end, the public sector took over a very large number of firms that had gone bankrupt and were about to shut down. The result was that by the early 1980s the large public sector holding companies were deeply in debt. When recovery from the recession finally came, there was a shift away from crisis management to a renewed emphasis on innovation and improving industrial competitiveness. Under talented new management, the public-sector holding companies sold off a number of firms to the private sector. By 1987,

IRI had successfully completed a very difficult transition. Having lost $1.9 billion in 1983, the company was now out of the red.[33]

Besides using public enterprises to promote employment and technological advance, a concerted effort has been made to promote Italian exports. The need to strengthen exports has been a function of the problems Italy has had in adjusting to a more open international economy and to very large changes in the terms of trade in recent decades. The trade liberalization resulting from Italy's membership in the European Common Market led to the first major push by government to assist exporters. Beginning in 1961 and enhanced in 1967, preferential credit was arranged for exports and for construction projects carried out abroad by Italian firms. About 80 per cent of these benefits went to the auto and machinery sectors in the 1960s and this proportion grew even larger by the late 1970s.[34]

During the late 1960s and early 1970s, Italian growth, like that in West Germany and Japan, was export-led, with most of the export gains being made by the efficient, large scale industries of the North, industries which were able to use exports to promote greater efficiency and rapid productivity improvements. Large scale exports helped Italian industrialists close the productivity gap between Italian and foreign industry. When the terms of trade turned against Italy in the mid-1970s, large Italian firms suffered in their export performance and the country came to rely on exports of traditional labour intensive industries such as clothing, footwear and furniture.

Assistance to small exporters has overlapped with assistance to small business in general. Small and medium-sized firms received a very large proportion of public-sector preferential loans and investment grants until 1973 (over 30 per cent), while after 1974 the proportion fell sharply to 13.9 per cent, as greater effort went into shoring up Italian exports and taking failing firms into the public sector.[35]

Small firms in Italy have always played a key role in the country's economy. They have been noteworthy for managerial flair and for flexible manufacturing in which companies produce customized products. One noteworthy example of the talent for customized production is the arrangement by which Pininfarina, the industrial designer and manufacturer, actually produces the body for Cadillac's new convertible, the Allente. In a unique operation, the company builds the bodies in a specially designed small plant adjacent to the Turin airport. Three times a week a jumbo jet flies the plant's total output, amounting to 8,000 bodies a month, to Detroit.[36]

In a broad sense, Italy's economic development since the Second World War has been a large success. To have progressed from the position of a semi-agricultural country to an advanced industrial nation which is on par with Britain in its aggregate output has been an enormous achievement. The shortcomings of the Italian economy, however, have remained all too obvious. The development of the South in relation to the rest of the country has been only a partial success. Still plagued with higher unemployment, a relatively poor economic infrastructure and a fragile industrial base, southern Italy continues to look at the rest of the country across a yawning cultural and social gulf. A graphic example of this division — when Palermo in Sicily, a city of 700,000, undertook a crackdown against the Mafia in the mid-1980s, some workers protested, carrying signs that read "Long live the Mafia" and "The Mafia Provides Jobs."[37]

The competitiveness of Italian industry is continually fragile. The country faces a very high government deficit, perennial balance of payments problems and the constant danger of renewed inflation. While social peace has characterized management-labour relations since the recession in the early 1980s, no one is sure that there will not be a return to the inflamed industrial scene of the 1970s. Moreover, there remains a major problem of lack of training in the Italian labour force for the jobs that are now being created in the economy.

In sum, Italian industrial strategy has been, to a considerable extent, defensive in character, protecting the country's industry against both enduring domestic structural problems and the volatility of the international economic situation. Despite these important reservations, however, Italy has grown as well as any country in Europe in the past quarter-century. Its development has made it an important factor in the shifting international balance of economic power which is underway.

Chapter Eight

Sweden: The Little Giant

Sweden is not noteworthy because of the size of its economy. In a world where large economies count for a great deal, Sweden is important because of the quality of its economic ideas and because its economic life casts an interesting light on the practices of other countries.

Sweden has pursued an economic strategy which, in essential respects has been the opposite of that of the United States. While the United States has sought competitiveness by holding down the cost of labour, Sweden has maintained the goal of full employment, has assumed that labour costs will be high, and has sought competitiveness through adoption of advanced technology and industrial restructuring.

The State and the Economy

From the mid-1970s to the mid-1980s, Sweden has managed a massive shift in its manufacturing sector, while keeping unemployment extremely low in comparison with other countries. Employment in the traditional sectors such as steel and textiles was halved in a decade, a transition which would have subjected many societies to enormous internal tensions. While far from problem-free, the restructuring was made socially acceptable by massive government support to minimize disruption in affected regions and industries. As traditional industries were phased down, growth shifted to industries with a better market potential, industries where technological upgrading could be undertaken — "engineering sectors" such as transportation, automobiles, and electrical and non- electrical machinery. There was also a marked expansion of the information technology-based industries which came to employ as many as 150,000 Swedes by the mid-1980s.[1]

On another front, Sweden's deployment of new labour-saving technology has put the country in the forefront of the industrial world. In 1974, Swedish industry deployed 1.3 industrial robots for every 10,000 people employed in manufacturing, a lower per-worker use of robots than that in Japan (1.9 per 10,000 employed). By 1981, Sweden led the field, deploying 29.9 industrial robots for every 10,000 manufacturing employees, compared with Japan (13.0), West Germany (4.6) and the United States (4.0). In 1983, this country of only 8.3 million inhabitants was making use of 1900 industrial robots, more than were France, Britain or Italy, countries with over 50 million inhabitants each.[2]

Sweden's technological achievement flies in the face of the conventional economic wisdom of the English-speaking countries. In the United States and Britain, the accepted view is that a powerful trade union movement is a major barrier in the path of economic progress. Strong trade unions, the argument goes, tend to keep labour costs rigid (by not allowing them to fall) and to block the introduction of new technology to protect the jobs of their members. The Swedish experience illustrates an alternative model, one in which organized labour has a very strong voice and in which comprehensive social programs, instead of causing high unemployment, provide the context for the introduction of new technology.

Let us further explore the Swedish economic model and how it differs from the approach in English-speaking countries. The wisdom of the English-speaking countries is that "Big Government" robs the economy of efficiency, introducing structural rigidities that make technological progress very difficult. It is further the view that expensive social programs are a luxury which an economy faced with serious external challenges cannot afford.

Sweden, with the biggest public sector of any industrialized country and with welfare programs that are among the most generous anywhere, has operated on radically different assumptions. The Swedish system assumes that it is precisely in periods of marked economic uncertainty and dislocation that it is most important to maintain extensive social programs. Strong social programs, including a major emphasis on worker re-training, are seen as a way to reduce trade union resistance to the introduction of new technology. Instead of assuming — as American and British workers characteristically have —

that new technology threatens their jobs, the Swedish trade union movement has been active in pushing for the deployment of new technology. Because the welfare state has been crucial in fostering this attitude on the part of labour, it has been an essential ingredient in the advance of the Swedish economy.

To understand how these principles have been applied in Sweden, we will trace the main features in the development of the country's economy for the past several decades. Sweden began its career as a centre for unorthodox economic experiment in the 1930s when the country's Social Democratic government initiated a counter-cyclical fiscal policy — pumping public funds into the economy to take up the slack during the Depression — well before Keynesianism became fashionable elsewhere. The Second World War of course, also created an important distinction between Sweden, which was neutral during the conflict, and all the other countries which were involved in the war and which emerged from it as winners or losers.

In the newly reorganized post-war international system, with its emphasis on increasing openness of trade and capital flows, Sweden was to play the role of a small industrialized country whose fate would be determined by its ability to be competitive. Sweden's counter-cyclical approach succeeded in keeping the country on a remarkably even economic keel so that growth rates varied only very slightly during the 1950s.[3] During that decade Sweden's GDP grew at an average rate of 3.4 per cent a year, below the average for OECD Europe (4.8), but ahead of the United States (3.26) and Britain (2.66).[4]

To stabilize investment flows in the economy and avoid alternating periods of strong and weak investment, Sweden introduced a scheme in 1958 that was novel in the industrial world. Under this investment funds system, firms were entitled to set aside 40 per cent of profits, and to deduct these funds in calculating their taxes. Provided that these funds were later invested during a time period stipulated by the government, they would remain free from profit taxation and a further 10 per cent tax deduction would be allowed. The purpose of the scheme was to maximize investments during economic downturns and it was such times that were designated for the earmarked funds to be invested. The system likely had the effect of increasing total investment as well as steering investment into critical time periods [5] (Since historically Swedish rates of investment have been satisfactory in comparison to rates in other industrialized countries, the Swedish experience indicates that a tax system with peaks and valleys — a high

general level, and lower levels for firms pursuing desired objectives
— can compete effectively against systems with low levels of tax.)

Sweden's rate of GDP growth advanced during the 1960s to an
average of 4.6 per cent a year, putting the country's expansion behind
that of France and Italy, on a par with that of West Germany, but ahead
of that in the United States and Britain.[6] During that decade the
Swedish government increased its expenditures significantly, but the
public sector still ended up with strong surpluses.

In the next decade, however, the Swedish economy veered sharply off course, forcing serious rethinking about the Swedish "model" —
a rethinking which has borne fruit in the much more favourable
economic performance of the country by the mid-1980s. Like other industrial countries, Sweden was hit hard by the oil crunch of 1973. The
terms of trade turned sharply negative, and the country entered a period
of mounting trade and government deficits and high inflation; GDP
growth tumbled to an average of 2 per cent a year over the decade.
Ironically, given the reputation of socialists as "big spenders," it was
while the Social Democrats were out of office from 1976-82 that the
country's non-socialist government massively increased public spending to protect jobs. The central government's deficit shot up from 2 per
cent of GDP in 1976 to 13 per cent by 1982. A good deal of the extra
spending by government was aimed at preventing failing shipyards and
steel works from going under. Between 1975 and 1982, government
subsidies to industry increased 17-fold to $2.4 billion.[7]

Again ironically, when the Social Democrats returned to power
under Olof Palme in 1982, they sought a strategy, "a third way," that
would allow Sweden to avoid either fighting inflation through higher
unemployment, or preserving jobs by giving in to inflation and higher
national indebtedness. To this end, the Social Democrats were determined to cut public spending, allow ailing companies to shut their
doors, and to shift their industrial policies from propping up industrial
dinosaurs to promoting the rapid transition to high technology.

Since 1982 the Social Democrats, have managed to wrestle the
central government's deficit back down to just over 4 per cent of GDP.
Along with this cut in the deficit, two factors have helped Sweden turn
its economic performance around — the decline in the international
price of oil, and a series of devaluations of the Swedish currency, the
krona (Kr), totalling 45 per cent of its value between 1977 and 1982.
Of course, the government could hardly take credit for favourable
economic developments, such as the change in oil prices, just as the

former government could not be faulted for negative external developments. What the government could take credit for, however, was the elaboration of an economic model which combined enterprise and intervention so as to avoid both high unemployment and high inflation.

Having already noted one of its striking achievements, the very rapid deployment of industrial robots, let us examine the major elements of Swedish industrial strategy in the 1980s. The push to expand the use of industrial robots has not been an isolated phenomenon. It is part of a general drive to move the economy toward higher technology, a move in which research and development has had a central role. Two agencies of the Swedish government have provided direct funding to support industrial R and D projects:

- The Board for Technical Development (STU) gives grants to support the early phase of R and D by industrial firms. If the R and D project leads to successful product innovation, the grant is repayable. In 1983, 220 million Kr went to such efforts, while twice that amount went to support basic research.

- The Industry Fund supports large-scale, long-term R and D projects carried out by major enterprises. From 1977 to 1983 the Fund has invested 1700 million Kr, with a fairly high success rate.[8]

Supported by these direct sources of funds, as well as by a variety of other fiscal measures, Swedish industry has undertaken a remarkable research and development effort. In 1983, Swedish R and D (both public and private sector) amounted to 2.3 per cent of GDP, putting it close to the top level among the industrialized nations.[9] In the same year R and D accounted for almost 10 per cent of total industrial value added, a rise from 4 per cent in 1973. Four industrial sectors achieved R and D components above 10 per cent — precision instruments 12 per cent, transportation equipment 16 per cent, electronics 18 per cent and pharmaceuticals 36 per cent. Sweden's R and D effort, which is mostly financed by industry, backed up with grants and subsidies from government, is overwhelmingly carried out by large enterprises, with 95 per cent of the effort being made by firms with more than 500 employees.[10]

The significance of Sweden's R and D commitment is that it has been the life blood of the country's evolution away from traditional industries to sectors in which the "brain" component is very high. This has allowed Sweden, with its marked dependence on exports, to search out those international market niches in which quality and custom manufacturing are more important than price. In a world in which there has been an intense competition and overcapacity in low and medium technology industrial products, this emphasis on flexible manufacturing and high technology has allowed Sweden to defend the competitiveness of its high wage economy.

Swedish competitiveness internationally is critical to the maintenance of the country's social system, which is the true purpose of its integrated web of economic and social policies. Sweden's social structure turns on an apparent paradox: the country has the world's strongest unions and a welfare state which is among the most advanced and, at the same time, it is home to a host of the most enterprising, privately owned multinational corporations.

Volvo, Ericson and Electrolux are three of the country's best known, highly successful firms. While Sweden is very much their home base, these companies sell 70-90 per cent of their production abroad.[11] About a third as many people are employed by the foreign subsidiaries of these Swedish multinationals as work for them at home. During the 1980s, about three-quarters of the total investments of the twenty most multinationalized firms have been made abroad. Foreign investment by Swedish firms has been largely motivated by the desire to gain and safeguard important overseas markets. Twenty-five to thirty per cent of direct investment abroad, most of which has been made through the direct purchase of foreign enterprises, has been located in the United States.[12]

This multinational component of Swedish industry is the leading edge of the country's participation in the international economy. What is remarkable in light of such competitiveness is the extent to which the country maintains its commitment to the other side of the Swedish paradox — powerful labour unions and the welfare state. More than 90 per cent of Sweden's blue-collar workers are unionized, as are 75 per cent of white-collar employees.[13] The country's collective bargaining system, which is highly centralized, has been very successful in facilitating contracts between labour and management without resort to strikes and other forms of industrial action. Bargaining takes place at intervals of one to three years between nationwide labour organizations and the Swedish Employers' Confederation (SAF), or other employer organizations representing governments, cooperatives and private companies outside SAF. In this process, the first step is to negotiate framework agreements on wages and working conditions. Then national unions sign collective agreements with employer associations. Job security and increasing worker input into corporate decision making have been key items on the negotiating agenda during the 1980s.[14]

During the last several decades, Swedish collective bargaining has succeeded in narrowing the wage gap in blue- collar industry. In the late 1960s, the gap between the highest and lowest paid blue-collar workers was 30 per cent, but by the mid-1980s it had become an astonishingly low 15 per cent. In addition, the average youth wage in blue-collar jobs had climbed to 75 per cent of the adult wage, up from 56 per cent of it in 1960.[15]

According to the conventional economic wisdom in the English-speaking world, such egalitarian wage policies should lower worker motivation, reduce labour mobility and increase youth unemployment. Indeed, unemployment amongst youth in Sweden is twice the national average — but at 6 per cent, it is vastly lower than the rate in the rest of Western Europe where it stands above 20 per cent. Moreover, a study by the Brookings Institute concluded that labour mobility in Sweden is as high as it is in the United States, measured by the percentage of people who change jobs each year. In addition, a study by the Centre for Labour Economics at the London School of Economics determined that Sweden has the most "flexible" labour market in any of the eighteen OECD countries, in its capacity to respond to economic shocks.[16]

The State and Society

The Swedish welfare state also challenges accepted economic wisdom in the English-speaking world. "Big Government," the conventional theory goes, is the enemy of economic success. But this has not been true in Sweden, even though the costs of maintaining the country's social programs have been considerable. Sweden's welfare state is the product of high taxation, of a tax system which is steeply progressive. The top marginal tax rate on personal income, of 80 per cent, is reached at an income of $46,000 a year — making Sweden's the highest taxes on an individual's income in the world. Naturally, with marginal tax rates that high, there is a strong inducement both to avoid taxes altogether and to take advantage of any available deductions to lighten the load. There are estimates that the black economy in Sweden could range as high as 10 to 20 per cent of GDP. Furthermore, the rich in Sweden have learned to reduce their tax load substantially by making use of tax deductions. As *The Economist* noted: "Once income from capital is taken into account, the progressivity of the tax system looks a lot less draconian."[17]

Despite the loopholes and the black economy, however, Swedes pay very high taxes. What do they get for them?

Swedes are provided with a system of universal national health insurance. Should a person be ill and have to stay at home to look after sick children, he or she is entitled to a taxable daily allowance, covering about 90 per cent of lost income. Health insurance also covers almost all fees for hospitalization, prescribed drugs and visits to doctors at public outpatient clinics. The system pays, as well, a large proportion of the fees of private doctors and covers about 40 per cent of dental fees.

Swedish parents receive generous assistance for childrearing. They are entitled to twelve months paid leave from their jobs following the birth of an infant. Either parent or both are eligible and six months of the leave may be saved and taken at a later time, prior to the child's eighth birthday. Tax-free child allowances are paid to all parents until their children reach sixteen. To supplement these programs, Swedish municipalities have been expanding the availability of low cost, public daycare for children. In addition, the school system provides children with free lunches and text books, and free instruction is available for the 25 per cent of Swedes who attend university.

To protect workers, Sweden has:

- a national unemployment insurance system, which covers most people, and, in addition, for those not covered, a system of cash benefits paid by the government.

- a national work injuries insurance scheme which pays all health insurance costs for those involved in accidents on the job.

- a noteworthy system of job retraining and special job creation which involves 4 per cent of the country's labour force. These programs assist people in moving from job to job as a consequence of technological change. They are also designed to combat long-term unemployment, which has been such a curse in the rest of Europe, by keeping people in contact with the working economy. While political leaders in all industrialized countries have talked about retraining of those affected by technological change, their efforts have been on a token scale alongside these Swedish programs.

Even though Sweden has a very extensive welfare state, it is far from having the highest level of state ownership of industry in the advanced industrial world. About 90 per cent of Swedish industry is privately owned, a much higher proportion than in France or Italy. The Swedish public sector includes services such as the post office, telecommunications, railways and electric utilities. In addition about twenty-five manufacturing companies are owned by the state holding company, Procordia. To put this in perspective, the Procordia companies have an annual turnover of about $1.5 billion compared with Volvo's (the biggest firm in Sweden) at over $12 billion a year.[18]

Many observers have found it curious that, with a Social Democratic party in office for most of the period since the mid-1930s, there is so little state ownership in Sweden. In fact, precisely because the Social Democrats were credited with leading the country successfully out of the Depression of the 1930s, many of the reasons for public ownership that were potent in other Western European countries were absent in Sweden. Following the war in Britain and France, nationalizations were undertaken both for ideological reasons and to help rebuild economies that had been ravaged. In Sweden, the Social Democrats had been in power throughout the war, and since the country had remained outside the conflict, there was no wartime devastation to be overcome. The Swedish tradition of strong government interventionism and of consensus-making between unions and private enterprise already existed and, to a considerable extent, obviated the pressure and the need for public ownership of industry.

Instead of public ownership, Sweden has developed an interventionist system whose purpose is to steer the economy through economic cycles and long-term technological changes. Effective economic power is held by partners in a tripartite system in which the private sector, labour and government are all effectively involved. By the mid-1980s, this Swedish system had shown itself adept at handling a difficult transition from one set of industries to another, while keeping unemployment low.

The longevity of the Swedish model does not mean that there has been no evolution within it. Most important, the Social Democratic government has moved far from Keynesianism which at one time was a mainstay of Swedish policy. As noted, in the period from 1982 to 1986 the government emphasized reducing the public-sector deficit as proportion of the GDP. Instead of expanding internal economic demand, as the Mitterand government did when it came to power in France in 1981, the Swedish government fostered programs to keep the nation's industry competitive and relied on currency devaluation and the resumption of foreign demand to get the Swedish economy moving again. At the end of 1986, the OECD placed Sweden's per capita GDP at just under $16,000 a year, only a little behind that of the United States and Japan, but ahead of that of West Germany.[19] The Swedes have shown that a small, independent industrial nation can compete in the world effectively while maintaining the integrity of its internal social system.

Chapter Nine

Canada: The Search for a Role Model

The seven major capitalist industrial nations have established an exclusive club of which they are the only members. Canada, despite the fact that its prime minister attends the annual summit meeting of the club every spring, is something of an odd fish in its midst. Canada was not actually invited to the first meeting of the club, initially a group of six, when it was called together at the initiative of France in 1975. The following year, however, when the Americans hosted the second such summit, they invited Canada, which has participated in all the subsequent meetings.

What makes Canada an odd member of the club is not the size of its GDP, which is about two-thirds that of Italy or Britain, but the nature of its economy. Despite its status as a rich industrialized country, Canada has a resource-based economy to a greater extent than any of the other major economic powers. As an important trading nation, conducting 70 per cent of its trade with the United States (Canada and the United States have the world's largest bilateral trading relationship), the country is heavily dependent on the export of vast quantities of a short list of commodities. Forest products, paper, metal minerals, wheat, natural gas and assembled automobiles — exporting these products gives the country the means to sustain its very high level of imported manufactured goods.

The other great fact about the country's economy is the extent of foreign ownership in Canada. Indeed, Canada was the proving ground for many American corporations when they made the jump from na-

tional to multinational status. Over one-seventh of all American investment outside the United States is located in Canada. American corporations, the key foreign investors in Canada, have invested there for two
main reasons: to acquire Canadian resources; and to gain access to the
Canadian market.

The country's historic reliance on the export of primary products
and the predominance of American-owned branch plants in the
manufacturing sector have had a decisive role in determining the structure of the Canadian economy. So powerful have these forces been that
they have played a major role in shaping the country politically and
culturally, as well as economically.

Canadians have always been strongly influenced by economic
thought in Britain and the United States. In recent years, American
economic orthodoxy, with its insistence on the virtues of free enterprise
and on the vices of state intervention, has had a major impact on
Canadian economic thinking. Historically, however, the building of the
Canadian economy has involved a large measure of state intervention.
Such intervention was needed to put into place the economic infrastructure to link together widely separated regions and to make possible a national economic existence in a country where a small
population lived in an immense territory. Yet today Canadians have
largely forgotten the essentials of their economic history in favour of
the truths of American economic thought. The major Canadian
response to the crisis of the global economy — a crisis which is a
product of American economic weakness — has been to draw closer
to the United States both in trade and in adopting the American approach to development.

The Historic Development of Canada's Economy

Canada was originally colonized by European countries as a source of
staple products needed by them. First, European fishermen appeared
off the Grand Banks of Newfoundland to make their catch for their
home markets. This exploitation of a colonial resource resulted in little or no permanent settlement. Next, came the quest for furs, a staple
trade that led to the settlement of New France, and conflict over
hundreds-of-thousands of square miles between competing French and
English commercial interests.[1] The conquest of New France in 1759
and the cession of the colony to Britain in 1763 made London the un-
disputed master of the Canadian fur trade. The American Revolution
cost the fur traders the southern part of their territory, the present

American midwest, in the peace treaty of 1783. Once the United States had come into existence, the northern economy was caught in what came to be its characteristic position, between Britain and the new giant to the south. Canada entered the 19th century with a fragile staples economy. Furs still mattered, but wheat and timber were becoming the key export commodities.

The colony's huge, ungainly economic system was centred at Montreal, where English merchants with a French Canadian labour force dreamed of a commercial empire that could compete with New York. The merchants were to fight a losing battle against their southern rival for the trade of the mid-continent. Before the political union of the British North American provinces in the Confederation of 1867, the Montreal merchants and bankers tried to make the most of the system of British mercantilism. However, when the mother country went over to free trade and threw the colonies into a new economic environment, the Montreal commercial interests sought close ties with the United States in the reciprocity agreement that operated from the mid-1850s to the mid-1860s. This, too, came to an end when the United States abrogated reciprocity because of tension with Britain during the American Civil War. Once again, the businessmen in the northern provinces had to search for an economic strategy.

This time, by default, they came up with a distinctive strategy which took several decades to develop and to bring to fruition. It was the boldest and most independent policy yet undertaken in Canada. But it remained, as strategies that came before and after, dependent on outside investment and on external markets for the country's staple products.

The economic logic of Confederation was expansion northwest into what is now the prairie provinces. Land-hungry farmers and ambitious bankers and railway owners gave Confederation its sinew. The economic promise of Confederation was realized only with the elaboration of what was called the "National Policy" at the end of the 1870s. Through the National Policy, the government of John A. Macdonald sought to develop industry in Canada. The strategy was simple enough. A protective tariff would limit foreign imports to allow products manufactured in central Canada to supply a larger share of the national market. (Soon the tariff would also encourage American firms to set up branch plants in Canada to assure their access to the Canadian market). The second element in the strategy, an all-Canadian railway tying the west to central Canada, would move the manufactured products to the growing market in the prairies and British Columbia. The railway would also carry the new staple product, western wheat, east to Montreal for export to Europe. For the strategy to work, the country needed more people, particularly in the prairies. Thus the third element in the National Policy was state-supported immigration from the United States, Britain and continental Europe.

The National Policy amounted to a partnership between business and government to bring into being an integrated national economy in which the scope for economic activity could be greatly enlarged. Without active government intervention, the national economy, comprised of interconnections between widely separated regions, would never have been possible. Canada took the interventionist route, not for theoretical reasons, but as a necessary consequence of the pressures of building a national economy in a cold country, larger in area than the United States, with a fraction of its population.

The National Policy, after several decades in which Canada's economic development was disappointingly slow, achieved its highest success in the first decade of the 20th century, when western Canadian wheat became the key national export. Transporting grain made the expensive national railway system successful and immigrants flocked to the prairies, thus greatly enlarging the market for central Canada's manufactured products. Rapid growth and the integration of the country's regions into a functioning national economy helped create a mood of buoyant optimism in Canada whose high point came in 1911, when Canadians rejected free trade with the United States in a national election, believing that their country would do better following the course it was on. That course had positioned Canada at the nexus of two very powerful external economic influences: one British, the other American. British investors had pumped very large sums into the development of Canada's economic infrastructure, most importantly, its railways, and, Britain continued to be Canada's largest trading partner. American influence, however, was increasing rapidly. By the eve of World War I, several hundred American corporations had established manufacturing subsidiaries in Canada. In these years, Canada was becoming the place in the British empire where the Americans did a significant amount of manufacturing.

Soon Canada was to be cast into a very different economic environment. The First World War upset the balance in the country's external relationships, greatly strengthening the United States while weakening Britain. During the interwar period, the wheat economy that had been at the centre of the National Policy became less important. In the 1920s a whole series of new north-south trading relationships developed. British Columbia forest products were shipped to American markets, as was Ontario, Quebec and New Brunswick pulp and paper. Metal minerals flowed to the United States from northern Ontario and Quebec, as did asbestos from Quebec. What did not change was the role of staple exports as the central dynamic in the economy. As in the past, shifts in the type of primary exports and in the destination of the exports determined the shape of Canadian economic evolution.

American mass production was unequalled in the world in the 1920s, as it was to remain for the next half-century. Steadily, over that time, Canada was drawn into an American economic orbit. The 1920s was the age of the motor car and pulp and paper. In that decade, American auto manufacturers expanded their facilities in Canada, producing vehicles not only for the Canadian market but for export to other parts of the British empire, such as Australia, New Zealand and South Africa. In world terms, 1929 was the high point for the Canadian auto industry. In that year, the Canadian industry produced over a quarter-of-a-million vehicles, of which more than one hundred thousand were exported.

The shifting focus of trade fostered a shift in political initiative within Canadian federalism. The federal government, the centre of intervention during the days of the National Policy, grew quiescent, while the provinces became much more important in economic matters than they had been. In the era of the motor car, provincial responsibility for road building suddenly mattered as much as federal power over railways had in preceding decades. Furthermore, the provinces owned the resources (with the important exception of the prairie provinces where resources were owned by Ottawa until the British North America Act [Canada's constitution] was amended in 1930.) The new north-south trade linkages established important economic empires for provincial governments. Queen's Park in Ontario presided over the Sudbury basin's vast nickel lode. Victoria, Quebec City and Fredericton held jurisdiction over huge forest product industries. Despite federal authority over international trade, Ottawa played a passive role in the development of American markets for these provincially-owned resources.

By the end of the 1920s, American investment and trade had surpassed British investment and trade in Canada. This trend continued during the Great Depression of the 1930s when there were numerous

American takeovers of bankrupt Canadian enterprises, acquired at bargain basement prices. During the Depression, however, power shifted back to the federal government. Provincial governments and municipalities faced bankruptcy and Ottawa's unlimited spending and taxing powers gave it new authority. Seven of the nine provincial governments gave up their own provincial police systems, hiring Ottawa to do the job instead through the Royal Canadian Mounted Police (the two exceptions were Ontario and Quebec). In 1940, the British North America Act was amended to give the federal government jurisdiction over unemployment insurance.

The Second World War accelerated the process of strengthening Ottawa's power vis-à-vis the provinces and greatly hastened the integration of Canada's political and economic regime with that of the United States. From the point of view of Canada's long-term future, the critical point in the war came in August 1940, during the Battle of Britain, when the Canadian Prime Minister, William Lyon Mackenzie King, drove the short distance from Ottawa to Ogdensburg, New York, to meet with American President Franklin Roosevelt. The brief meeting in the President's private railway car led to the announcement that the two countries would form a joint board of defence and a permanent military alliance. In this highly informal fashion, with no prior consultation by King of the Canadian cabinet or Parliament, Canada established a military alliance with the United States that was to become the country's key foreign link, one that soon supplanted the relationship with Westminster in importance.

Canada emerged from the war a major industrial power, its military production having been a massive success. Paradoxically, while the war pulled Canada and the United States closer together politically and economically, it also made Canada a stronger industrial nation, less dependent on American investment than at the beginning of the conflict. In the end, however, what counted for Canada was the closeness of its relationship with the United States and the shared world view of its leaders with those in Washington. The end of the Second World War was a key point in the evolution of Canadian policies. As in the era of the National Policy, the country was at an economic crossroads, requiring a basic choice of direction. For the Liberal government of Mackenzie King, it was natural enough to base post-war economic policy on still closer ties with the United States, not least because of that country's immense power in the global economy. In 1945, the federal government decided to end the direct role it had played in the productive sectors of the economy during the war. Many publicly-owned facilities were sold to the private sector at low prices. Instead, Ottawa would undertake a reconstruction policy with two essential elements: a commitment to full employment and equitable social programs for Canadians and an open door to U.S. investment to fuel economic growth.

In Canada, the adoption of Keynesian demand management policies to counteract the booms and busts of the market economy was to be closely related to the emergence of the welfare state. The idea was that when demand lagged, government was to stimulate the economy with tax cuts and direct public-sector spending. Then, when the economy was in danger of overheating because full employment had been reached, government would increase taxes and cut its own spending to prevent an inflationary spiral. Much of the public-sector spending that would provide ballast for the economy took the form of outlays for social programs: family allowances, hospitalization, medicare, pensions and unemployment insurance.

If Keynesianism was to give Ottawa the tools to fine tune the economy's trajectory, it was American investment that would guarantee takeoff. U.S. investment poured into the manufacturing and resource sectors of the Canadian economy, an economy in which American subsidiaries played a crucial role. Initially, the branch plants promoted growth and higher employment, which disguised their other, more negative, consequences. By increasing the dependency of Canadian manufacturing on imported technology, machinery, and parts and components, the branch plants gradually undermined the ability of Canada's industries to produce commodities from start to finish. In addition, as with previous Canadian economic strategies, the branch-plant economy depended on the export of primary and semi-fabricated products to keep the country solvent in its international transactions. To the list of products exported in the 1920s, the important post-war additions were to be oil and natural gas.

Boom and Bust

To most Canadians, the potential shortcomings of the branch-plant economy were not a major concern. Indeed, the era of the 1950s and 1960s, would later be remembered with nostalgia as a golden age of prosperity in Canada. Closely tied to the heart of the American economic system, Canadians prospered as the American system prospered. In the period from 1960 to 1968, Canada's real GDP grew at an average rate of 5.6 per cent a year, making the country third in growth among the seven major countries, behind Japan (10.4), and Italy (5.7), but ahead of France (5.4), the United States (4.5), West Germany (4.1) and Britain (3.1).[2] Beneath the surface of this rapid growth, however, one could already see signs of future trouble. Among the seven major countries, Canada enjoyed by far the most rapid rate of population increase during these years, an average of 1.9 per cent a year, as compared to 1.1 per cent a year for the seven countries taken together.[3] The growth in Canada's real GDP per person employed, during the period from 1960 to 1968, was 2.7 per cent a year, putting the country at the same level as Britain (2.7) and the United States (2.6), but well behind the other major countries — Japan (8.8), Italy (6.3), France (4.9), and West Germany (4.2).[4] Canada's economy was growing in size, but qualitatively its growth in productivity was on a par with Britain and the United States and well below the others.

Canada's branch-plant economic strategy began to unravel in the early 1970s. Yet the first step away from the strategy had been taken several years before — with the signing of the Canada-U.S. Auto Pact in 1965. The Auto Pact was a limited free trade agreement between the two countries, allowing the producers of assembled vehicles and auto parts to ship their products duty-free across the border, provided that they met certain minimum production requirements in Canada. The Canadian government entered into the Pact as a way of rationalizing the inefficient and uncompetitive branch-plant automotive industry. The problem with the branch-plant industry had been that each of the major American auto manufacturers had produced a full line of cars in Canada, cars to be sold in the Canadian domestic market. In effect, the Canadian auto industry had been a miniature replica of the American industry and, as a result, had been denied the benefits of economies of scale. Given this uncompetitive industry, the Canadian government had considered two choices: rationalization of the industry to produce a limited number of vehicles from start to finish for the Canadian market; or continental integration, the production of car parts and assembled vehicles for segments of the entire North American market. Under the Auto Pact, the Canadian government chose the latter option.[5]

With the Auto Pact, Canada's largest manufacturing industry moved from behind a tariff wall to a new continental arrangement. The rest of the branch-plant economy was to be altered by two sets of developments: the weakening of the United States in the global economy; and the impact of tariff reductions as a result of successive rounds of GATT negotiations.

On August 15, 1971, as already recounted, U.S. President Richard Nixon took a series of steps to increase American competitiveness in the global economy. The United States abandoned the gold standard, established a temporary 10 per cent surcharge on imports, and began a process of forcing the downward revaluation of the dollar against other currencies. All these steps were taken to shore up America's position against the other major industrial powers. One additional step was to have an important effect on Canada. The Nixon administration initiated a tax scheme, the Domestic International Sales Corporations (DISC), which allowed companies to write off 50 per cent of their taxes on products which they exported. DISC was especially important to Canada as the largest trading partner of the United States and the country in which the largest concentration of American foreign investment was located. As an export subsidy to American firms, DISC enticed them to supply their branch plants abroad with machinery and parts produced in the United States. The result was a heightened tendency for American firms to cut back on their actual production facilities. A study published by the Foreign Investment Review Agency (FIRA) in Canada in 1982 revealed that non- Canadian firms (mostly American) included an import component in their products that was three to four times that of domestic firms. Measures such as DISC were a sign of the new aggressiveness in international trading in which both defensive and offensive measures were used to preserve home markets and to invade foreign ones. When deployed by the United States, such measures helped break down the already crumbling walls of what was left of the old National Policy in Canada, a policy that had left Canada with its own separate, albeit subsidiary, economy.

Tariff cutting has also promoted the integration of the Canadian and American economies. By 1967, there had been seven rounds of GATT negotiations, and the most recent one, the so-called "Kennedy round," had resulted in an average reduction of industrial tariffs of about one-third. The next round, the "Tokyo Round," was completed in 1979. Under the agreement which came into effect on January 1, 1980, Canada committed itself to reduce its tariffs by about 40 per cent in eight equal reductions to be completed on January 1, 1987. By the end of the process, Canada's tariff on dutiable industrial goods was to drop from just over 14 per cent to just over 9 per cent; furthermore, most of the products traded between Canada and the United States would do so duty-free. (This was not the same thing as free trade, however, since as tariffs became less important, non- tariff measures, with significant trade effects, became ever more significant.)

As tariffs were cut, the distinction between imported and domestically produced goods became blurred by the practices of American companies; Canada was being pushed into a new and uncertain economic environment. For a time, however, the country's economy performed well enough that the new economic realities could be ignored. Canadian economic growth slowed after the oil crisis of 1973, but less than in most of the other major industrial countries. From 1973 to 1979, Canadian real GDP growth averaged 3.4 per cent a year, behind that of Japan (3.6), but ahead of France (3.1), the United States (2.6), Italy (2.6), West Germany (2.3), and Britain (1.5).[6] Canada's strength as a petroleum producer helped to shield it against the shock felt throughout the industrialized world. It benefitted from higher export prices for oil and natural gas and kept its domestic petroleum price significantly below the new world price, thus shielding industry from the sudden change. While Canada's real GDP growth dropped from 7.5 per cent in 1973 to 3.5 per cent the following year, its 1974 performance was much better than the average of the major countries, a dismal 0.1 per cent.[7] In 1975, Canadian growth bottomed out at 1.1 per cent, still ahead of the average of the big-seven of -0.4 per cent.[8] Again in the recession at the end of the decade, Canadian growth reached a bottom of 1.0 per cent in 1980, ahead of the big-seven average of 0.9 per cent and the United States at -0.4 per cent.[9]

The next recession in 1981-82, the most severe since the Depression of the 1930s, was to be different. In 1982, Canada suffered the most severe downturn in any of the major countries at -4.3 per cent, worse than that in the United States (-3.0) and the average of the big-seven (-0.7).[10] The recession took a heavy toll throughout Canadian society. Young people coming into the job market found themselves facing the stone wall of unemployment. Between January 1981 and December 1982, the number of jobs held by young men (aged fifteen to twenty-four) fell by 272,000. The unemployment rate for young men soared from 13.5 per cent to 24.0 per cent. Between the peak of employment in 1981 and the trough in 1982, 321,000 jobs were lost in the nation's goods-producing industries, 194,000 of these in the manufacturing sector. Business bankruptcies reached record-breaking levels. Every part of the country was affected, from Newfoundland, where real levels of unemployment (including discouraged workers) climbed far past 20 per cent, to Alberta, where the petroleum boom ended and unemployment reached more than 10 per cent.

The nature of the Canadian recovery from the recession made clear just how vulnerable the country's economy had become. In regional terms, the Canada of the 1980s was a very different place from the Canada of the 1970s. In the previous decade, it had been the resource producing areas, particularly Alberta with its oil and natural gas industry, that had done well. Indeed, in the 1970s, there had been a steady migration of population from east to west. Recovery from the recession of the early 1980s, however, coincided with low prices for resources and in particular, with falling petroleum prices. International oil prices began to fall in early 1982, later plunging dramatically to as low as $12 a barrel in 1986. Under these conditions, the previously favoured West remained in the economic doldrums during the recovery which was centred in Ontario and Quebec.

The main engine of recovery was the booming American automobile market. Canadian auto exports increased prodigiously, becoming the nation's most important export. Exports of transportation equipment (almost entirely assembled vehicles and auto parts) soared to $31 billion (Can.) in 1984, out of the nation's total exports of $82 billion (Can.).[11] Salomon Brothers in New York estimated that 33 per cent of the growth in Canada's economy in 1984 was the direct result of exports to the United States, of which automotive exports had become the largest component.[12]

Relying on the auto industry as the major engine of growth had obvious drawbacks. Auto exports would hold up as long as did American auto demand, not only for autos in general, but for the specific mix of models assembled in Canada. The problem was that the auto industry was notoriously cyclical, the first manufacturing sector to decline in the event of an economic downturn.   Moreover, the buoyant auto market of the mid-1980s was subject to obvious long-run vulnerability. If oil prices rose again sharply, as many experts expected they would by the early 1990s, the auto industry could be a large loser. To compound matters, in the late 1980s, the Japanese automotive industry is still making gains over its North American competitor, and the likelihood is that its share of the American and Canadian auto markets will continue to rise (subject of course, to buffeting by American protectionism). What Canada's share of the continental auto market will be like in the 1990s, when the Japanese will have become major producers of vehicles in new North American plants, is far from clear.

Finally, the rapid advance of robotization of auto plants is bound to have a negative impact on employment in the Canadian auto industry, an industry in which the strong component is assembly rather than parts. It is in assembly plants that jobs are being lost to robots. While taking short-term advantage of the auto boom made sense for Canada, the longer-term horizon is not so favourable for the auto sector.

Canada's greater dependence on the automotive sector was matched by growing dependence on imports of high technology manufactured products. During the 1970s, the proportion of imported research-intensive manufactured products used in Canada increased from 43 per cent to 54 per cent. During the 1970s, Canada's self-sufficiency in such products declined from 77 per cent to 71 per cent. In an economy with a very high degree of foreign ownership, it was natural that new techniques and new products were conceived elsewhere and then exported to Canada. Branch plants had always carried out little research in Canada, and particularly when it came to major innovations, the important research was done elsewhere.

Added to this problem is Canada's dependence on American companies for new technology and industrial techniques during the period of American industrial decline. When the United States had been the paramount industrial power, Canada's branch-plant economy had been less disadvantageous. The country's industries were next door to the source of the world's most advanced technology and techniques. With American decline, however, Canada is the neighbour of an industrial metropolis which is no longer foremost.

The outlook for Canada's economy in the late 1980s is one in which vulnerability looms large, vulnerability that takes the following forms:

- Soft demand for raw materials and low petroleum prices means that the traditional primary-products sector of the Canadian economy is weak, with serious implications for major Canadian regions. Recovery can be expected, particularly in the petroleum industry over the medium term, but large parts of Canada seem fated to continue riding the roller-coaster of a "boom-bust" economy.

- Dependence on the auto sector for recovery makes the country's economy susceptible to future unfavourable developments there.

- Canada's research and development performance is among the poorest in the industrial world, a legacy, to a considerable extent, of the branch plant economy in which American subsidiaries have relied on their home operations for new technology.

- General Canadian growth after the recession was closely tied to the strength of American demand. The proportion of Canada's exports going to the United States increased despite the fact that the American economy was declining in terms of global importance.

These vulnerabilities, coupled with the fact that the traditional branch plant economy was becoming a thing of the past, have generated a crucial debate in Canada on the course of economic development. The debate centres on whether Canada should negotiate a comprehensive free trade agreement with the United States, a proposal that became the key economic program of the Progressive Conservative government of Prime Minister Brian Mulroney in the fall of 1985.[13]

While the debate was touched off by free trade negotiations, it is really about much more than that. It is a debate about what kind of economic strategy makes sense for Canada in the late 20th century. Should Canada adopt an economic course like that of the United States, more "market driven" than in the past, so that its economic practices would conform sufficiently to those south of the border to make a North American free trade area viable? Or, should Canada, relying on the experience of its own interventionist past, and learning from the current enterprise-intervention models being pursued in other countries, seek a new industrial strategy and a global trading option?

In 1987, the country's economic elite is largely united around the notion of further economic integration with the United States. Given Canada's poor record in productivity growth and its dependence on industries that tend to represent the past rather than the future, and given the country's very close integration with the United States in terms of trade and American investment, it is not unreasonable to expect it to follow the general trajectory of the other major English-speaking countries in the late 20th century.

Chapter Ten

The Soviet Union: Will "Glasnost" Help?

In global terms, Soviet economic power has declined even more dramatically than has American economic power since the end of the Second World War. Indeed, Americans can take comfort in the fact that sustaining superpower status has subjected the social and economic system of their major adversary to enormous strains. The period of reform of Soviet economic and social life, inaugurated by the General Secretary of the Soviet Communist Party, Mikhail Gorbachev, is symptomatic of the failure of the Soviet system.

There are important respects in which Gorbachev is a Soviet counterpart to Ronald Reagan. Each of them looks back for inspiration to the 1920s, Reagan to the good old days of free enterprise, Gorbachev to the New Economic Policy (NEP) initiated by Lenin. Each has sought to rid his system of debilitating later influences, Reagan of the New Deal legacy of the welfare state, Gorbachev of the legacy of Stalinism. Each leader has set out to achieve a "restoration," overcoming the problems of the more recent period by seeking inspiration in the more distant past.

The need for Soviet economic renewal is beyond dispute. In the late 20th century, the Soviet Union is falling behind the most advanced industrial nations, in both qualitative and quantitative terms. The technological gulf has been widening as a result of the extraordinary technological revolution of the past two decades. Soviet officials, having long denied the importance of the micro-electronic revolution, are now conceding that crucial advances have been made and that their country has been left behind. In quantitative terms, Soviet failure is no less dramatic. At the end of the Second World War, Soviet analysts looked forward to the time, thought to be several decades away, when their economy would pass the American as the world's largest. Instead, by the year 2000, the Soviet Union's economy is almost certain to fall behind that of Japan in absolute size. The Soviets face the very real prospect of having the third largest economy in the world — not all that far ahead of West Germany's in absolute size, and technologically inferior as well — by the first quarter of the next century.

The "Command" Economy

The Soviet Union has a command economy in the sense that the major decisions about production and pricing are taken by the state rather than through a market system which responds to consumer demand. Soviet economic planning can be characterized as "directive," meaning that management is obliged to follow plans set out for it, in contradistinction to the "indicative" planning practised in many Western European countries, where a strategy is adopted for the economy which firms are enticed or prodded to follow.

Agencies of the Soviet state make tens-of-thousands of decisions on what products are to be produced and at what prices they will be sold. The crucial planning arm of the Soviet government is Gosplan, the state planning agency, which has overseen the preparation of a long-term plan for the Soviet economy from 1976 to 1990 and which takes account of the economic development of the countries allied with the Soviet Union. Gosplan also prepares the more operational Five Year Plan, for example the 11th Five Year Plan which covered the period 1981-85 and presented detailed growth targets for the economy in both sectoral and regional terms.[1]

Sociologist David Lane has described the process of developing the Five Year Plan and its scope as follows: "The plan is concocted after the working out of problems by the various committees and discussion in the party and government apparatuses. The Five Year Plans include detailed projections for economic enterprises, with targets or 'control figures' for developments during the five year period with breakdowns by year. These cover production and sales, investment, wages and labour, profit, incentives, technical developments and productivity, and a financial plan. The details are worked out in consultations between the various committees, the bank and the ministries to which the enterprise is subordinate."[2]

Soviet planning has concentrated power in the hands both of top bureaucrats and of the leadership of the Communist Party. Enterprises in the Soviet Union are not analogous to those in the West in the sense that they are not autonomous entities. A Soviet firm is an operating branch of an industry, in which top executive power is exercised by a government ministry. The manager of the firm, while he has some freedom to decide on the mix of products in his plant, cannot make the decision to produce a new product, and cannot respond to changes in the pattern of demand in society.

The relationship in the Soviet economy between top bureaucrats and the party, the other major focus of power, is by no means a simple one. In principle, the reason for state ownership of the overwhelming bulk of the means of production is to allow the Soviet economy to be run for the benefit of the whole society rather than for the profit of private owners and managers. To give this principle substance, the Communist party, in theory the instrument of working class power, must have the power to guide the state bureaucracy to ensure that the production of goods and services is for the benefit of all.

In practice, however, the party's role is more restricted. The party does play a key role in putting together the Five Year Plans. But because the directives to enterprises and whole sectors of the economy are based to a large extent on the data provided by the bureaucrats who run particular industries, there is a tendency for the bureaucrats to end up as the authors of their own instructions.

In the past twenty years, there has been a gradual decentralization of power in favour of the managers of enterprises, giving them somewhat more room than formerly to decide on the mix of products their units produce. Incentives have also been increased so that if firms exceed their production quotas, the wage and benefit packages for the workers can be improved. While decentralization has increased the power of managers somewhat, their position is in no way comparable to that of the management of Western firms. Soviet enterprises remain units in a system in which the most important decisions are made higher up.

Soviet trade unions also play a role very different from that of their Western counterparts. Their ability to represent worker discontent is severely restricted in both theoretical and systemic ways. The reason for the theoretical constraint is that the Soviet Union is a socialist state in which the whole governmental apparatus is controlled by the Communist Party in principle, on behalf of the working class. According to

Marxist theory, there are no class contradictions in Soviet society and, therefore, no fundamental conflict between worker interests and those of management. While there are occasional wildcat strikes in the Soviet Union, strikes are not led by official unions. Indeed, it is one of the jobs of unions to maintain discipline in the work place. This does not prevent unions from representing the grievances of individual workers in cases of wrongful dismissal and inappropriate discipline. Such grievances are aired in labour-management boards, where decisions can be appealed to the courts.

In addition to fighting grievances and negotiating wages and benefits, unions are responsible for administering some social programs, running cultural and athletic activities and overseeing on-the-job safety measures. Soviet unions are also charged with responsibility for helping firms to meet their production quotas. As part of their duty in furthering the collective aims of the enterprise, unions are supposed to be on the lookout for corruption and illegal profiteering. Indeed, it is not unusual for the manager of a Soviet firm to lose his position as a result of charges against his conduct being brought by union officials.

While Soviet unions represent workers in ways which are analogous to the operations of Western unions, they are constrained both by the role they play in effect, as part of management (responsible for personnel), and by the Soviet theory of decision-making and democracy. Soviet decision making operates on the principle of "democratic centralism." Under this system, trade unionists — like the Communist Party — elect their leaders, but the leadership then plots the course which the membership as a whole is required to follow in a disciplined and obedient fashion. Operating on the basis of democratic centralism, and closely interlocked with the Communist Party, particularly at the upper levels, the Soviet trade union movement is definitely not autonomous like the now outlawed Solidarity union in Poland was.

Democratic centralism, of course, has implications for the Soviet economy and society as a whole; it determines that essential communications in Soviet institutions flow in one direction only — from the top down. The system suffers enormously as a result of the lack of feedback from below. A self-sustaining elite gives orders and hears far too little about the morale, the conditions of work and the attitudes of those who must carry out the orders. The decades-old problems faced by Soviet society as a result of this system of decision making have been described by economic historian Alec Nove: " ... the new men [the managers and bureaucrats] were remarkably indifferent to the welfare of the masses ... Petty officials, managers, army officers, disregarded the most elementary needs of their subordinates to a degree almost past belief, in a country supposedly under a working-class dictatorship."[3]

The Origins of Centralism

To see how the Soviet system became highly centralized, and the implications this has had for Soviet economic performance, we will review the major stages in the country's economic development.

The Bolshevik revolution of 1917 brought to power a party that had spent its entire previous history plotting the overthrow of the Tsarist regime, and very little time planning how to use state power, let alone how to run an economy. The First World War, the period of the revolutions and the subsequent civil war weakened the country's economy, greatly undermining its heavy industrial sector and even dispersing much of its working class, the social force on which the revolution most depended for success.

Even after the initial success of the revolution, there was no great rush to think about the long-term development and structure of the economy. The Bolsheviks, including Lenin, were optimistic that the October revolution would soon be followed by others in the advanced industrial nations, particularly in Germany. These revolutions would make the Soviet Union a large, but still backward, element in a much wider move to socialism. It was many years before the Soviet leadership realized that world revolution was out of the question, and that what lay ahead instead was "socialism in one country."

While the Bolshevik regime moved quickly to bring many of the country's major industries and banks under state ownership, the shape the Soviet economy was to take remained highly uncertain until the end of the 1920s. How much capitalist enterprise to allow and what to do about private ownership of farmland were the two central debates of the era.

Before the New Economic Policy was inaugurated in 1921, Lenin had pursued a policy of comprehensive nationalization and centralization. This policy was not the result of any thoughtful strategy. It was rather the outcome of desperate circumstances — of severe food shortages and confiscation of the peasants' grain surpluses, of chaotic seizures of industrial property, of experiments with workers' control, of government nationalizations. This spasmodic development went by the name "war communism." To some, war communism, which included the movement toward a moneyless economy, appeared to be a rapid route toward true socialism; actually, during its brief ascendancy, the country was careening toward collapse. By 1921 industrial output had declined to 31 per cent of its 1913 level.[4]

The move back toward a more mixed economy under NEP was taken by Lenin for reasons of economic realism, not principle. He was facing up to the fact that the productive system was on the edge of collapse. NEP began by abandoning the practice of confiscating agricultural produce; instead it introduced a tax in kind and later a money tax. Farmers were allowed to market their produce and this quickly spread to other sectors where private marketing of consumer goods was re-established — a move away from the extremism of the earlier period and the re-establishment of a money economy. Decrees in the spring and summer of 1921 revoked the nationalization of all small-scale industry and allowed people to undertake private handicraft production and to set up small-scale industrial operations involving no more than ten to twenty workers.[5]

The NEP system gradually reduced the country's enormous problems. Reaching its peak in 1924-25, private business grew significantly until it came to dominate the country's retail trade and much of its small-scale industrial production. In addition, at the peak of the NEP system, agriculture was almost wholly in private hands.[6] NEP led to fairly rapid growth, to an improvement in living standards (perhaps back to the levels of 1913) and to a high degree of tolerance toward the peasantry. While there was state ownership of major industries (Gosplan had been established in 1921), there was as yet no "command" economy in the sense that there would later be in the Stalin era.

The transition from NEP to the highly centralized, state-owned economy of full-scale Stalinism was not sudden. The late 1920s and early 1930s were the transitional years during which attacks on the NEP system increased and the drive for massive industrialization began, linked with an increasingly coercive political regime. Why the leaders of the Soviet Union turned against NEP during this period is a complex question. One reason has to do with their innate hostility to all forms of capitalism — after all, the Bolsheviks had not carried out their revolution to make Russia a haven for small business. But there was more to it than ideology. By the late 1920s, the illusion that the revolution of 1917 was the beginning of a world revolution had faded, to be replaced by the fear of capitalist encirclement. If the Soviet Union was going to have to make it on its own, then it would have to be a fully viable, self-contained industrial giant, capable of repelling any possible military attacks from the outside. The slowly dawning realization that the Soviet Union would have to industrialize on its own, with no help from more advanced countries fresh from their own revolutions, opened the door to Stalinism.

It is not our purpose to discuss the paranoia, the purges, the liquidation of foes, the building of the totalitarian state that was the essence of Stalinism; here our aim is rather to note the essentials of the economic strategy of Stalinism. The demise of NEP can be seen in the decline of the private sector in the Soviet Union, from 42.5 per cent of total trade in the country in 1924-25 to 5.6 per cent in 1930, from 54.1 per cent of national income in 1925-26 to 9.3 per cent in 1932.[7] At the same time, taxes on private business and well-off farmers (kulaks) were sharply increased and private business was proscribed by laws making speculation a criminal offence.

Stalinism was coterminous with the era of the Five Year Plans whose goal was the industrialization of the country on a gigantic scale. Huge amounts of capital were directed into mining, steel making and electric power projects whose benefits would be distant and whose immediate effect was to lessen consumption and to exacerbate the shortage of consumer goods. Paralleling the effort to industrialize was the enforced revolution in the countryside, in which private farming was replaced by collective and state agriculture. (In passing, it should be noted that the destruction of the kulaks through confiscation of their land, exile, separation of families, starvation and mass murder is one of the great tragedies of the 20th century.)

Giving the whole economic strategy a set of precise goals was the first Five Year Plan of 1928 — the result of a colossal effort on the part of Soviet thinkers and bureaucrats.[8] With the launching of the plan, Gosplan became a much more important entity. The drive for industrialization, the central purpose of the Five Year Plan, was to be achieved through a massive alteration not only of the economic structure of the country but of its society as well. Stalinist industrialization was inextricably linked to the forced collectivization of the peasantry. By 1936, 89.6 per cent of peasant households had been collectivized. The strategy of the Stalin regime was to squeeze the peasants, beyond the point of starvation if necessary, to accumulate the capital for industrialization. Whether the system actually worked is debatable.

While surplus was wrung from the hands of the peasants so that millions starved, the repressive means employed by the regime actually caused a sharp decline in agricultural output. Given the lack of reliable statistics for the period, it is impossible to conclude whether more was obtained from the peasants through coercion than would have been obtained through the continuation of the NEP-style policies.[9]

Industrial expansion itself was driven by the same disregard for any priorities except those of the regime. Haunted by the belief that the Soviet Union needed to catch up with the industrial capacity of the advanced countries within a decade, Stalin was relentless in increasing the goals of the Five Year Plan, and then on insisting that they be met in four years instead. Professor Nove has noted the result: "The 'Stalin' model was created in the process of trying to do the impossible, and therefore, by facing everyday the necessity of assuring supplies to the key projects or 'shock constructions', at the expense of others regarded as of lesser importance."[10]

It is impossible to separate any discussion of the Soviet economy in the 1930s from the political atmosphere of the time. Planners and economists were among those subjected to the merciless and savage reprisals of Stalinism. Their Plans and projections were regularly attacked as deliberate sabotage, as "wrecking," as anti-Marxist. Many such people ended up facing the firing squads of the Stalin terror. Under the circumstances, it is an understatement to say that creative debate about the shape of the Soviet economy and society ended once the various "oppositions" to Stalin — whether Trotskyist, Bukharinist or whatever, had been eliminated. The staggering long-term cost of the Stalinist method of industrialization was the stifling of intellectual and institutional autonomy. It was to hobble the Soviet economy for half-a-century.

Still, there can be no question that in the 1930s Stalinism produced results, particularly in the development of the country's infrastructure and heavy industry. After the terrible year of 1933, investment and production grew and food rationing was ended by stages in 1935.[11] Growth in heavy industry was very rapid during the second Five Year Plan, which began in 1932. Strong industrial expansion in a number of key sectors was helped by the "Stakhanovite" movement, an effort by workers in factories and mines to increase productivity through their own efforts.

In 1937, however, expansion was interrupted by the "great purge," the orgy of execution and exile directed by Stalin against imagined and real political opponents and against anyone unfortunate enough to be suspected of "wrecking" or sabotage. The result again was to undermine the honest efforts of talented planners and to create an atmosphere in which submission supplanted creativity.

The third Five Year Plan, begun in 1938, aimed at a very large increase in the output both of industrial and consumer goods. As the threat of war loomed ever larger, before the German invasion on June 22, 1941, productive efforts were shifted to the manufacture of military hardware. In this last period before war, discipline in the work place was made even more draconian than in the past. Workers were prohibited from changing jobs without official permission. Absenteeism from the job was made a criminal offence for which workers were imprisoned, including, in some cases, pregnant women or mothers whose only crime was to stay home with small children.[12]

By the time of the German invasion, the essentials of the command economy were in place in the Soviet Union. Soviet survival during the conflict depended heavily on the enormous achievement involved in shifting whole industries east of the Ural mountains out of the reach of Nazi armies. The war left twenty million Soviet citizens killed, and twenty-five million homeless. At its end 1,710 towns and 70,000 villages were designated "destroyed." It was no exaggeration to say that the western half of European Russia and almost all of the Ukraine and Belorussia were wrecked. While millions of soldiers came home after the war, often with new skills equipping them for work in industry, millions, of course, never returned, leaving widows and orphans to rebuild their lives and their communities.

The Post-War Record

Not surprisingly, the immediate post-war years were devoted to rebuilding shattered industries and cities and re-establishing farm production in devastated regions. During this last period of Stalin's life, the essential features of the command economy, in the words of Alec Nove, "became frozen into their pre-war mould."[13] Gosplan was charged with the task of devising a fourth Five Year Plan whose goal was to bring Soviet economic output back to its pre-war level by 1950. Reconstruction was aided substantially by the insistence on reparations from defeated countries, including Hungary, Bulgaria and Rumania, but especially Germany, in the form of the wholesale transfer of industrial plants to the Soviet Union.

Although reparations helped, the process of re-industrialization was largely owing to the efforts of the Soviet people themselves, and was particularly successful in the field of heavy industry. The Stalinist antagonism toward the peasantry continued, however, and Soviet agricultural output improved only very slowly in the late 1940s and early 1950s, a period in which unproductive collective farms and state farms — the former owned in common by those who worked them, the latter owned by the state — produced the vast bulk of the country's food. Stalin still granted higher priority to vast "showpiece" industrial projects and buildings than to the expansion of industries producing consumer goods, or to the building of living accommodations to overcome the country's appalling housing shortage. Moreover, as the Cold War intensified, the tendency to favour basic industry and military output was reinforced.

Oddly enough, given the Soviet planning fetish, there was an important bias to Soviet economic development that was to have very important long-term consequences. Stalinist planning, with its persistent emphasis on the surpassing of production quotas and its preference for the gargantuan, was oriented overwhelmingly to the quantitative at the expense of the qualitative. The incessant demand for increased production encouraged managers at every level to concentrate on turning out more of the same rather than on innovating. The problem with a shift to new products, or to a new balance among the goods made, is that such innovation is initially destructive of existing capital investment, requiring new machinery and the learning of new techniques. In an atmosphere where failure was often rewarded with imprisonment or even death, few managers were likely to be innovators. The result was cumulative failure by Soviet industry to make the qualitative advances being achieved elsewhere. The qualitative weakness of the Soviet economic performance was exhibited in its backwardness in areas such as chemicals, plastics, synthetics and natural gas — sectors where great advances were being made in the West.[14]

Soviet economic policy since the death of Stalin in March 1953 has involved periods of reform and decentralization and periods of quiescence and recentralization — but, while the extreme political repression of the Stalin era has receded somewhat, its basic economic model has remained intact. Changes to it since the death of Stalin have sometimes reformed, but never transcended, the model.

The key figure in the period of reform that followed Stalin's death was Nikita Khrushchev, who became the First Secretary of the Soviet

Communist Party and ended the brief ascendancy of Georgi Malenkov. Khrushchev's first major initiative was the overhaul of Soviet agriculture. He recognized that the peasantry had been squeezed on the collective farms through low payment for their produce, high taxes and low investment in agriculture. The result, Khrushchev understood, was low farm productivity. To improve the lot of farmers, to improve their morale so that production would increase, the government raised the prices received by collective farms for their output, took over some of the costs of shipping produce to market, and cancelled debts owed by collectives to the state. In addition, the taxation paid by peasants for production on their own private plots was reduced, a measure designed as an incentive to increase this form of production. (Later, much of this trend toward a better deal for farmers was reversed, when collective farms were saddled with onerous charges for the purchase of agricultural machinery.)

Beginning in 1957, there was a major push to convert collective farms to state farms — sometimes through pressure from above, sometimes voluntarily at the initiative of the leadership of collectives who were hoping for more investment in their operations if they converted to state ownership. Khrushchev's agricultural policies were aimed at overcoming the legacy of Stalinism: the inability of the Soviet Union to feed itself; and the necessity to use a much higher proportion of its workforce on farms than did the advanced countries of the West.

Like other Soviet leaders, however, Khrushchev was lured by the gargantuan. He launched a massive effort to increase the amount of land on which grain was grown and a campaign for the large-scale conversion to corn production in the European sections of the U.S.S.R. Khrushchev's grain offensive centred on bringing enormous new areas of land in northern Kazakhstan, southern Siberia and southeastern European Russia into grain production under the auspices of state farms. Cultivated land in the Soviet Union was increased by 40 million hectares between 1953 and 1956, most of it on the fringes of adequate rainfall. It was to be a mixed blessing for the country's economy, increasing its farm output in years of good weather, and imposing a new burden on it in the form of wage payments during the years of drought that were all too frequent in such regions. Similarly, Khrushchev's enthusiasm for corn often led to large-scale conversion on land that turned out to be unsuited to such use. While his agricultural campaigns increased the country's farm output somewhat, they failed to come to terms with the central problem of Soviet agriculture, the low productivity of collective and state farms in the large parts of the country where superb levels of output should have been possible. In other words, Khrushchev tried to solve the problem of Stalin's legacy by expanding the scale of agriculture (a quantitative solution) rather than by addressing the qualitative issues and so opening a debate about the model on which Soviet agriculture was based.

Khrushchev tried as well to improve the performance of Soviet industry. A large number of reforms, beyond our purpose to discuss in detail here, were undertaken. One of the most important was the attempt to shift much of the country's planning from a sectoral to a regional locus by increasing the importance of the economic ministries of the republics within the Soviet Union. This reform was responsible for sowing considerable confusion, since it greatly increased the problem of how much production of a particular kind of commodity, from a particular facility or region, was needed elsewhere in the country. Problems of this sort were, of course, inherent in a command economy, in which production was undertaken in response to administrative instructions rather than market demand. Khrushchev's efforts to change the framework for issuing instructions for production did not alter the essential nature of the command economy, but did cause confusion — over-and under-production of given commodities — as well as providing scope for profiteering by industrial managers, a problem dealt with by the introduction of the death penalty for profiteering in 1961.

Despite the difficulties, there were definite successes. Soviet industry increased its output and the standard of living of the Soviet people rose perceptibly. (It should be stated that reliable statistics for the Soviet economy have not been available, so that when we note a rise in living standards, it is not possible to do so with the same precision as in the case of western economies.) In the period 1958 to 1965, according to Soviet sources, general industrial targets for expansion were met — in the case of steel, targets were exceeded — while quotas for machine tools and synthetic fibres were not met.[15] A great psychological moment for the regime was the launching of Sputnik in October 1957, the first satellite to orbit the earth, an achievement which deeply shocked American society and which gave the whole world the sense that the Soviet Union was at the frontier of scientific advance.

With all his reforms and counter-reforms, structural innovations and cancellations, Khrushchev gave the appearance of a leader desperately trying to breathe life into a system whose main characteris-

tic was a tendency to revert to stagnation. The frenetic, circular character of the regime, the product of a wilful and inconsistent intelligence,
was a major reason for Nikita Khrushchev's fall from power in October 1964. The hectic Khrushchev years were followed by the era of
Brezhnev and Kosygin, during which structural restoration was the
main theme. In this period, agriculture continued to be a weak link in
the Soviet economy, despite the move away from twists and turns in
policy of the kind that had been characteristic under Khrushchev.
While farm output increased on the whole, despite setbacks during
years of drought, the goal of making the country self-sufficient in food
production was not realized. And because the real incomes of the
population were rising while food prices were kept artificially low,
there were perennial shortages of meat and fresh vegetables. Unproductive by the standards of the West, Soviet agriculture was under-
capitalized and agricultural equipment all too often was subjected to
rapid wear and tear. As the country expanded its herds of livestock to
increase meat production, grain production proved inadequate to supply enough feedstock to support the herds and dependence on imported
grain grew.

Weak agricultural performance held back the Soviet economy in
two important ways. First, too high a proportion of the country's work
force was involved in the production of food, in comparison to performance levels in the West, thus denying other sectors of the economy
the potential for new labour input. Second, lack of self-sufficiency in
agriculture caused a perennial trade deficit in food which forced the
Soviet Union to export other commodities such as oil to earn the
foreign exchange to pay for imported food.

Industrial stability and growth were further goals of the post-
Khrushchev regime. Structural reforms were undertaken to place more
power in the hands of the managers of particular enterprises, while at
the same time, responsibility for overall planning was shifted back to
the central government from the republics. Many earlier reforms were
reversed, the industrial ministries were reinstated and Gosplan became
once more the crucial planning agency.[16] The Soviet economy expanded from the mid-1960s to the mid-1980s, although the rate of
growth decelerated after the early 1970s.

However, to refer to the slowing of growth only in a general sense
glosses over specific developments that were important. While Soviet
industry grew during the three Five Year Plan periods from the mid-
1960s to 1980, the country's production of consumer goods and food

fell far below the projected targets. Production bottlenecks, unnecessary duplication of effort, failure to develop technologically — these were important features of Soviet economic performance. Analysing the failure to meet targets in the tenth Five Year Plan, which ended in 1980, Alec Nove commented: " ... only gas and passenger cars reached their five-year targets. Other sources of energy, and also steel, fertilizer, tractors, many other items of civilian machinery, locomotives, building materials, and virtually all consumers' goods, were far behind expectations." He added: " ... growth has shrunk to modest levels, and the system is creaking at the joints."[17]

One reason why the Five Year Plans prior to 1980 succeeded better at the aggregate level of national output than in meeting targets for a wide range of key commodities, was the very high level of military spending during the period. Estimating the level of Soviet military spending is no easy matter since Soviet and Western claims regarding it differ so greatly. In the West, Soviet statistics on the proportion of the nation's economic output devoted to the military are dismissed as absurdly low when the extent of the Soviet armed forces and military hardware is taken into account. Soviet figures claim that, for 1971-75, military spending accounted for 9.5 per cent of output and that the proportion dropped to 6.6 per cent for 1976-80, and declined still further to 5.3 per cent in 1982. The CIA, estimating defence costs and investment and research devoted to defence, put the military effort at 11 to 13 per cent of output in 1970, and placed it at 13 per cent in 1982.[18]

Whatever the correct figure is, it is not unreasonable to conclude that military spending saddles the Soviet economy with a very onerous burden, a burden which is even more severe in qualitative than in quantitative terms, since so much of the country's best scientific and engineering talent has devoted its efforts to military output. While the Soviet command economy has proven itself a cumbersome and inefficient instrument for providing Soviet citizens with the goods they want, it is set up to ensure that military hardware is supplied.

One of the political goals of American military spending in recent decades has been to force the Soviet Union to spend so much on defence that it will be unable to meet its targets in other areas such as consumer goods. Whether one regards the Soviet Union as an expansionist power that has undertaken very high military spending as a matter of preference, or as a country pressured into military spending by the American defence effort, it is clear that the high proportion of resources devoted to the military has created severe problems for the Soviet economy.

Before we go on to assess the implications of the Gorbachev reforms for the Soviet economy, we will consider how well the economy has performed in recent years. Such an assessment is again subject to the limitation that widely different claims on the performance of the U.S.S.R. have been advanced in the Soviet Union and the West.

Official Soviet figures have put the annual percentage growth of the economy at 7.4 per cent a year for the period from 1951 to 1980. The CIA estimates Soviet growth for the period at an average of 4.7 per cent a year.[19] Obviously, the different implications of the two sets of figures are large. The Soviet figure puts the expansion of the U.S.S.R. almost as high as that of Japan, while the CIA estimate puts it well behind Japan's growth, in the range of West Germany, Italy and France, while ahead of that of the United States and Britain.[20] Since the Gorbachev regime has itself been vigorously attacking past Soviet statistics and calling for more reliable ones, there is little reason for us to have much faith in the ones so far available. The CIA figures suffer from possible bias and also from the fact that making external estimates of the performance of a country whose own statistics are suspect is no easy task.

What is less controversial than the Soviet Union's long-term average economic growth is that Soviet expansion has been slowing down since the early 1970s. Both Soviet and CIA statistics agree on this. The CIA estimates that Soviet economic growth has declined in the following manner over the past two decades: 1961-65 — 5.9 per cent a year; 1971-75 — 3.7 per cent a year; 1976-80 — 2.7 per cent a year.[21] In the spring of 1987, the CIA and the U.S. Defense Intelligence Agency issued an estimate that, following a decade of growth at rates just over 2 per cent a year, Soviet growth had climbed to 4 per cent for 1986. The study attributed the spurt in expansion to the best Soviet grain harvest since 1958. It forecast growth between 2 and 3 per cent a year until 1990, below what it described as Gorbachev's "implied goal" of 4 per cent a year.[22]

Some idea of how far the Soviet economy has come in recent decades can be gleaned from comparisons of the Soviet and American supplies of particular commodities. In the mid- 1970s, while there were 53 telephones for every thousand people in the Soviet Union, there were 627 telephones per thousand people in the United States. The figures for other commodities per-thousand population in the two countries were as follows: radios — Soviet Union 211, U.S. 1965; television sets — Soviet Union 182, U.S. 474; cars — Soviet Union 12, U.S. 448.[23] Also helpful is a comparison of how much of an average worker's labour time was necessary to purchase particular items. In the Soviet Union, it required 701 hours of an average industrial worker's labour to make the money to purchase a colour TV in 1982. In the United States, only 65 hours of a worker's labour was necessary to make the purchase. Again, while it required 53 months of a Soviet worker's labour time to finance the purchase of a small car in 1982, it required only 5 months of an American worker's labour to pay for a similar car.[24]

Focusing on these commodities, of course, tells only part of the story. Defenders of the Soviet economy point out that the U.S.S.R. has virtually full employment and a system of social welfare, free education and publicly funded health care — making those aspects of Soviet economic performance superior to that in the United States. Low cost rent in the Soviet Union meant, for example, that while the Soviet worker laboured only twelve hours to earn his monthly rent money, an American worker toiled for fifty-one hours to do the same.[25]

While conceding something to the rejoinder, it is not unreasonable to conclude that for a country that has placed a high priority on industrial achievement and whose ultimate socialist raison d'être has been the well being of its people, the Soviet economy has been a failure. Evidence of corruption, low morale in the workplace, the production of shoddy commodities, interminable shortages of meat, fruit and vegetables, crowded housing conditions, long queues in front of shops as a part of daily routine — these features of Soviet economic reality are now being pointed out regularly in Moscow as well as in the West.

What impact, then, can the reform policies of Mikhail Gorbachev have on the structure and performance of the Soviet economy?

Under the banner of "glasnost" (openness), Gorbachev has set out to reform the Soviet economy and Soviet society. Throughout this book, we have concerned ourselves with long- term economic trends, leaving short-term fluctuations or very recent events as largely outside our investigation. In the case of the Gorbachev reforms, an exception needs to be made. In the short period since he has held office, Gorbachev has stirred hopes and anxieties in a way that no Soviet leader has since the death of Stalin. What concerns us is why the Gorbachev reform is under way, the nature of that reform as far as the economy is concerned, and whether reform is likely to improve Soviet economic performance.

On the first point, it is clear that the Gorbachev program results from a perception of just how wide the gap between the Soviet economy and that of the West really is. It reflects the realization that the micro-electronic technological revolution, often dismissed in the past as unimportant by Soviet leaders, has left the Soviet Union dangerously backward and falling further behind at a rapid pace. At the same time, Gorbachev's policies are based on the desire to find ways to open up the Soviet economy to new sources of talent and creativity, to the pressures of public criticism, and to the potential for greater initiative at the level of particular enterprises, while maintaining the essential principles of the Soviet command economy and the political rule of the Soviet Communist Party.

There are inherent tensions within this set of goals. Opening up the Soviet political and economic system necessitates greater reliance on public opinion — whatever forms that takes. And public support for reform will depend on success, in the not too distant future, in greatly improving the Soviet economy for consumers — something the system has failed to do since its inception. Moreover, short-term success in producing consumer goods runs smack up against another Gorbachev aim — capital investment to upgrade the technological base of Soviet industry. Finally, while greater autonomy for individual enterprises may promote the well being of the Soviet economy in the long term, it cuts against the ability of directives from above to steer enterprises in the short run — and it must not be forgotten that the current impetus for reform comes from above.

To date, Gorbachev's main economic initiative has been a draft law, published for discussion in February 1987. The law would give workers a greater say in the management of enterprises and would make enterprises more responsible for showing a profit. Under the law, enterprises would have more say in determining how many workers they needed and how much they should be paid. (It is possible that money losers might, under some circumstances, be allowed to go bankrupt and close their doors.) Enterprises would also be empowered to do much more direct trading with each other than in the past. The concepts embodied in the draft law follow the experiments undertaken in 1983, whose most high-profile examples have been the Togliatti automobile plant and the Sumy engineering works. These experiments are said to be going well so far.[26]

Assessing the prospects for the Gorbachev reform effort is no easy matter. It is clear that Gorbachev faces enormous opposition, as he and his supporters have stated publicly, from powerful elements within the Soviet bureaucracy and Communist Party. It is also by no means obvious just how far Gorbachev and his followers intend to take Soviet society in their campaign for "glasnost."

There is no reason to doubt Gorbachev's word when he says that his aim is to strengthen the socialist system in his country and to take it further on the path to true communism. To see his policies as steps toward the economic and social system of the West is almost certainly a mistake. Gorbachev remains strongly committed to the essential principles on which the Soviet economy has been founded — state ownership of major industries and collective agriculture. The central question is whether the historic failure of the Soviet economy has been based on the system *qua* system, or on the corruption of the system that was the legacy of Stalinism. No one, of course, knows the answer to this question. It is not unreasonable to postulate, however, that the problem resides not in Stalinism alone, but rather in the over-centralization and bureaucratization that was implicit in the Leninist concept of the state and Communist Party from the start. That proposition will doubtless be debated for years to come and at great length.

However that debate turns out, we can reasonably assert that the Soviet Union is a declining economic power in the late 20th century, now involved in a desperate effort to catch up. On its perimeters in Western Europe and Japan are the economic powers which have been most successful since the end of the Second World War.

Conclusion

The Future of the Major Industrial Economies

From the end of the Second World War until the early 1970s, the international economic system devised by the United States worked well, even extremely well. Growth rates in the major industrial countries were never higher. However, since the early 1970s, the American-designed system has been in crisis, and since the severe recession of 1981- 82 none of the major industrial countries has achieved satisfactory and sustained growth. The Reagan administration in the United States has attempted to restore America to its former position in the system, but the result has been temporary growth, supported by an extravagance of imports and foreign borrowing. The American people are left facing slow growth and a mountain of international debt. Similarly, the Japanese and West Germans, the masters of export-led growth, have pursued their strategies to a point of diminishing returns. The other four major countries are reduced to pursuing strategies of short-term adaptation, while they wait for some clear initiative from the three pre-eminent economic powers.

Will there be an initiative, and if so, what form could it take? In this chapter, we will draw conclusions about the larger patterns of economic growth in the past four decades and speculate about the likely directions the years to the end of the century could take.

First, let us note what has worked well and what has worked less well in the countries under discussion since the Second World War. In this book, we have surveyed countries that have operated economies of three kinds: enterprise; command; and enterprise-intervention. Broad conclusions can be drawn.

The countries with enterprise economies, especially the United States, began the period after the war in the strongest position, but their long-term fate has been economic decline, relative to the rest of the global economy. The United States entered the post-war era with the following distinct advantages, which taken together, allowed it to exercise supremacy within the system: industrial superiority; an enormous surplus of capital for export; a large trade surplus; and military superiority. Of these four elements, the only one which remains intact in the late 1980s is military superiority. Trade and capital surpluses have been replaced with enormous deficits, and in key industrial sectors the United States has fallen behind its competitors. In a speech at Harvard University in the spring of 1987, Paul Streeten, a professor emeritus at Oxford University, argued that American post-war supremacy had been based on these four areas of advantage, and that the "Pax Americana" had broken down in the same way as the "Pax Britannica" broke down after World War I.[1]

The Soviet Union, the only country with a command economy we have analysed, entered the post-war period after a terrible war for national survival with twenty million of its citizens dead and much of its countryside and cities in ruins. Since the war, the Soviet economy has failed to make the advances that many Marxist theoreticians had expected. Having hoped to pass the United States and become the largest economy in the world, the Soviet Union is in point of fact likely to fall to number three, behind Japan, by the end of the century.

The countries that adopted enterprise-intervention economies were the cinderellas of the post-war epoch. They built their economies within the American international system. Japan, West Germany, France and Italy seized the materials that were at hand for reconstruction. While they launched enterprise economies with powerful private sectors, they could ill afford the assumption that the state was not key to economic well being. For all of them, state intervention was crucial to success. What emerged was a series of national economic experiments in very diverse cultural and social settings which were nonetheless united by common principles. In each case, the private and public sectors worked together as partners; the assumption that there was an antipathy between the state and the private sector did not exist to anything like the extent it did in the enterprise economies. In some of these countries, notably France and Italy, direct public ownership of industry was relatively more important; in other cases, intervention took the form of joint public-private planning, the use of state subsidies and tax breaks, support of technological breakthroughs through the creation of temporary cartels and co-determination of industry involving the trade union movement. Whatever the mechanisms, the principles on which intervention was undertaken were broadly similar and were applied by governments representing a diverse political spectrum from right to left. French Gaullists, Italian and West German Christian Democrats and Japanese Liberal-Democrats represented the conservative end of the spectrum. French, Italian and Swedish Socialists and Social Democrats represented its left component. The fact that enterprise-intervention economies have functioned under the political rule of both the right and the left suggests that they have rested on a social base in which major segments of business, the state bureaucracy and the working class have been united around key elements in a common agenda. In the cases of Japan, West Germany, Italy and France, what made these social alliances possible was the fact that at the end of the war the old, dominant segments of business were displaced and replaced with newer, younger business leaders who were forced to share power with the state bureaucracy, and in some cases with labour as well. In the three countries which were the major victors of the war, the United States, the Soviet Union and Britain (despite the victory of the Labour Party in 1945), the social framework was not significantly altered at the end of the conflict.

The enterprise-intervention economies have had the best results in terms of rate of growth and qualitative advance. The following figures for 1950 to 1982 measure their overall growth in real GDP per capita compared with that of the United States and Britain, the leading enterprise economies. From 1950 to 1982, Britain's real GDP per capita nearly doubled, in constant 1980 pounds, from 1,888 to 3,555. In the United States real GDP per capita was some distance short of doubling, increasing in constant 1972 dollars from 3,511 to 6,377. In the enterprise-intervention economies growth was much stronger. In France, real GDP per capita more than trebled over the same period, increasing in constant 1975 francs from 9,155 to 31,761. In West Germany also, real GDP per capita more than trebled, rising in constant 1975 DM from 5,741 to 19,578. In Italy, real GDP per capita again more than trebled, increasing in constant 1975 lira from 793.7 (000) to 2,697.9 (000). In these three cases, over a period of thirty years, real per capita GDP increased at almost twice the rate achieved in the

United States. Japan, of course, made the most impressive gains of all, increasing its real per capita GDP more than eightfold in constant 1975 yen from 207.6 (000) to 1,719.6 (000) between 1950 and 1982.[2] As a result of this rate of expansion, the enterprise-intervention economies have grown too large and too powerful for the present international economic system.

Why have the enterprise-intervention economies had the greatest success? This question involves many complex dimensions since we are examining the performance of quite diverse societies over an extended historical period. And yet, the superiority of the enterprise-intervention economies has been so sustained and so striking that it seems necessary to seek some answer, however general, to the question.

It appears that the enterprise-intervention economies have been superior to the others in two crucial respects: their capacity for planned technological breakthroughs and industrial advances; and their ability to involve a relatively high proportion of the population in economic decision-making.

The enterprise economies have tended toward a short-term, market orientation. American corporate management has developed a quarter-to-quarter bottom-line approach, fine for imitating, but not much good for innovating. The problem is that, particularly when it comes to developing new technologies or wholly new kinds of products, the market is a far from reliable guide. The Japanese demonstrated this fact convincingly in their development of industrial robots, leaving their competitors, who waited for the market to signal them, far behind.

The enterprise economies have used military spending as a back-door route to innovation, stressing the "spinoffs" that flow from military R and D into the rest of the economy. Consider these words from an address in the autumn of 1986 by Geoffrey Pattie, Britain's minister of trade and industry:

> Of course, SDI (Strategic Defence Initiative) is a defence research program with particular aims. But in its wake can come inventions and discoveries that can profoundly affect the lifestyles and aspirations of the people of the world. Think what can be achieved by a transport system which does not rely on fossil fuel; by reductions in the rate of destruction of tropical rain forests as a result of new materials; by marked reductions of pollution generally; by

improvements in agricultural practices thanks to better satellite imagery.

These are not pie-in-the-sky ideas. These are realistic objectives which will improve the everyday life of our global village. [3]

Rarely is the case for spinoffs put in such fulsome terms. However, the spinoff route to innovation is highly indirect, putting the countries that employ it at a considerable disadvantage vis-à-vis countries that use more direct means.

If the enterprise economies have suffered as a result of their short-term market orientation, they have also faltered because a relatively narrow segment of the population has been involved in economic decision making. In the United States, economic decision making is conceptualized as an interaction between the sovereign consumer and the servant entrepreneur through the medium of the marketplace. While the role of the consumers is far from unimportant, this economic model stresses the risk taking and activism of entrepreneurs. Entrepreneurs, and in the case of large corporations, managers in conjunction with top technical personnel, are the key legitimate economic actors in the society. State bureaucrats are seen as a negative force, constantly embroiling entrepreneurs in red tape and getting in the way of economic progress. Similarly, in this model, trade unions are seen in a negative light as a force that holds up technological advance, fights for the retention of outmoded jobs and saddles the economy with an unrealistic and rigid wage scale. Real economic actors in the enterprise economies tend to be the owners and managers of private-sector companies and their senior technical staff.

In the command economy of the Soviet Union, there is a bias in favour of the quantitative over the qualitative. This bias, which has also given the command economy a short-term orientation, has grown out of the constant battle for economic units to achieve quotas set for them by the state planning system. Decision making in the command economy is severely attenuated. Needless to say, entrepreneurs do not have much of a role — and given the top-down system of democratic centralism, neither do the workers. This is a system in which the real economic actors, as opposed to those on behalf of whom the economy is supposedly being run, are top political leaders and senior bureaucrats. Considering the severe political repression that has characterized so much of Soviet history, creative dissent from the views of the elite has hardly been encouraged.

The enterprise-intervention economies have been better at managing long-term technological breakthroughs and at involving a broader segment of people in their decision making. The planned advances in the production of computers and robots in Japan and the shift of the Swedish manufacturing sector from the steel and shipbuilding industries to R and D intensive manufacturing are two potent examples. Moreover, decision making in the enterprise-intervention economies has involved entrepreneurs and, in large corporations, managers and top technical staff, but it has also involved government bureaucrats, and, in some cases, trade unionists. While this is far from making these countries a nirvana of participatory democracy, it does mean that in the actual functioning of the economy, the number of active economic decision makers is larger. The input of workers into decision making on the job in West Germany, Sweden and Japan, and the planning process for industry as a whole, involving business and the state in Japan, Sweden and France, are examples.

In countries with enterprise economies, the assumption is regularly made that the democratic state is the enemy of the free economy. In countries with enterprise-intervention economies this assumption is less often made, and much less often acted upon.

Future of the Golden Triad

What does the future hold for the American-centred international economy? The heart of the advanced industrial world is comprised of a triad, a golden triad whose citizens enjoy the highest living standards in the world. The three parts of the triad are: the United States, with Canada on its periphery; Japan; and Western Europe. The United States has been the linchpin in the system — the economic, military and political power holding it all together. Today the United States may well lack the power to continue as a single, dominant force to unite the system. The crucial question is whether the system can be reformed under a new and broadened leadership, or whether the golden triad will begin to break apart into its constituent parts. To probe this question further, let us consider the parts of the unsymmetrical triad, to see what are the prospects for change.

The United States

The United States has reached a critical point in its national evolution. Having successfully integrated the international economic system since the end of the Second World War, it must now either promote the creation of a collective leadership for the advanced industrial world or move toward a greater degree of isolation.

There is little indication that Americans are in the mood for facing a choice of this kind, little evidence that they are even aware that such a choice confronts them. This is not to say that there are no perceptions in the United States that something has gone wrong. Many have pointed to the sliding of American competitiveness, to the rise of the international debt and trade deficit of the United States and to the on-going problem of Washington's deficit. The rise of Japan has painfully intruded into the American consciousness, but in a partial and distorted way. The tendency has been for Americans to express outrage at what has been seen as Japanese trickery in seizing so large a part of the American market while conceding so small a part of its own. The rise of Western Europe, less spectacular than the rise of Japan, has not imprinted itself on the American mind. The Europeans are still seen in patronizing terms by Americans as effete, as unwilling to arm themselves, as quibblers over the details of American foreign policy — not to be taken entirely seriously.

As far as economic renewal is concerned, the United States is pursuing its agenda of private enterprise and small government. Deregulation, the rise of small business and industrial restructuring are routinely perceived as the saviours of the hour.

It is difficult to measure the impact of deregulation, except to say that there has been little sign of improvement in American productivity, a strong indication that the industrial malaise has not really been addressed. And there have been ironies and unpleasant surprises with deregulation as well. The symbol of triumphant deregulation was the freeing of airlines nearly ten years ago from government controls over fares, routes and schedules. Now there is growing uncertainty about the safety of the system and there is all too much certainty about rising consumer discontent with late flights, and overbooking and cancellation of flights. In the spring of 1987, officials of the U.S. National Transportation Safety Board were warning about an alarming rise in midair near misses, a shortage of controllers to guide pilots, and complaints from pilots about poor maintenance of aircraft and about airliners flying even when important instruments have not been

154 Decline of the Superpowers

functioning.[4] Not surprisingly, deregulation has encouraged the airliners to bunch their flights at the most profitable times of the day,
usually those taking businessmen to their daily meetings in the morn-
ing and back home at supper time. As the *Economist* noted: "For example, Hartsfield airport in Atlanta, the country's second busiest,
which has four runways, cannot possibly land eight Eastern flights and
send off four more for Delta at precisely 7:25 p.m."[5]

In the ideological hothouse of deregulation, however, why should
government have any say in the times at which private airplanes fly?
Following this logic Ronald Reagan fired all the air traffic controllers
for their illegal strike in 1981 — one of the most popular acts of his
presidency, and one which illustrated the low esteem in which unions
were held in America. Before the dismissals, there were 16,375 controllers, 13,348 of whom were designated as fully trained. In the spring
of 1987, there were 15,089 controllers, 9,565 of them fully trained.
Moreover, by the spring of 1987, these controllers were handling 30
per cent more flights than were their predecessors in 1981. Now, while
businessmen, usually big fans of deregulation, found themselves in
holding patterns over congested airports, they could read newspaper
accounts of the controversy over air safety.

Deregulation has been a key feature of the American response to
foreign competition because it has strengthened the market and pushed
back the forces of government intervention. While the case that
deregulation increases efficiency has yet to be demonstrated, it is not
difficult to see how it may contribute to less safe travel, to worsened
pollution, and to decreasing standards of industrial safety. While
deregulation may be a good idea as a way of countering meddlesome
rules, the problem is that it has been undertaken, not merely for reasons
of practicality, but to make an ideological point as well. This ideologically motivated attack on the state has robbed the United States of use-
ful forms of government intervention, as well as ridding it of noxious
ones.

Small businesses have been seen as another key way for the United
States to renew its economic dynamism. Over the past decade small
businesses have created a very large proportion of new jobs in the
United States. Between 1975 and 1983, the number of people
employed in establishments of under twenty employees increased by
nearly four million. And the number of people employed in establishments with between twenty and ninety-nine employees increased
by more than four million. On the other hand, establishments employ-

ing more than one thousand workers increased their aggregate employment by less than seven hundred thousand during the same period.[6] While small businesses were thus crucial to increasing employment, their role needs to be seen in a broader context. American employment has been shifting away from the manufacturing sector to the service sector, from full-time to part-time employment, and, in many cases, from higher paying to lower paying jobs. The burgeoning of small businesses, heavily concentrated in the service sector, has occurred in a period when American competitiveness internationally has been declining and when the United States has been living beyond its means, relying on imports and foreign borrowing. When the day of reckoning comes for the United States, and the country begins to come to terms with its government and external deficits, the small- business sector will be placed under enormous pressure and there may well be a large increase in bankruptcies and in the number of small firms taken over by larger ones in a new movement toward corporate concentration. In a rigorous new study of the role of small business in the economy, Peter Johnson says that, given the high infant-mortality rate of new, small firms, and given the length of time it takes the survivors to grow, the impact of small firms on total employment is limited. He concludes that, at the end of any decade, 10 per cent, at most, of all employment is to be found in firms that started up during the decade. And he notes that not all the jobs in those firms can be counted as additions to the work force since some of them have been created at the expense of others in companies that were pushed out of business by the new competition.[7]

Industrial restructuring — trimming the fat off firms, by reducing workforces to the level where maximum efficiency can be realized, cutting inventories, making use of just-in- time supplying of industrial inputs — has contributed to the survival of American corporations in the difficult environment of the 1980s, an environment in which they have had to deal with severe recession followed by the massive problems caused by the overvalued dollar. Despite its undeniable importance, Harvard Business School Professor Michael Porter has written that restructuring is not enough: " ... restructuring is not a strategy. It is a means of dealing with the failure of past strategies. The strategic agenda for many companies is still unfinished. Now that the easy cutting phase is over, the real challenge is to build. This will involve the creation of new and lasting competitive advantages, and the development of new products and services."[8]

That statement could be taken to apply to the American economy as a whole and not just to individual enterprises. The emphasis in the United States on entrepreneurship as the answer to all problems has been overdone. It contradicts the history of what has succeeded best in the post-war period. In its hour of economic difficulty, Americans, more than ever, have emphasized the superiority of the enterprise system over all others. Such a state of mind will not make adjustment to reality an easy thing.

Adjustment will be difficult as well because it requires the recognition that while American power continues to be very great, it is limited in ways which were certainly not true a generation ago. Americans do not like to hear that sort of thing from their political leaders, as Jimmy Carter, who attempted to say it, discovered at the hands of a man who believed that America could be restored to its former pinnacle.

If a new international economic order must rest on an enlarged leadership, this means that the United States must consciously accept the need to share power with others. One can easily find daily advice from Americans, in government or in the media, to other countries. The Japanese and the West Germans have been regularly told to accept their share of economic leadership by reflating their economies. The Japanese have been urged to lend more money to the Third World, and have been badgered about importing more and exporting less. Advice is cheap, of course, and this is not what is meant by accepting the fact that a real sharing of power is needed. The Americans have also received plenty of cheap advice: to cut back on their oil imports in order to prevent OPEC from getting back into the driver's seat on oil prices; and to get their budget deficit under control by raising taxes.

To date, the United States has not taken external advice seriously, and that is one reason the annual meetings of the leaders of the seven major industrial nations regularly conclude with vague and unimportant joint statements. It is true that Americans have taken more seriously meetings with the Japanese, West Germans and sometimes the French and British to coordinate policy on exchange rates. The famous New York meeting of G5 in the fall of 1985 had an important effect on bringing the U.S. dollar down from its formerly unrealistic heights; but since the United States had already decided it wanted a lower dollar, this example does not indicate that the United States has given up its ingrained habit of acting unilaterally on key matters and forcing the others into line. The most successful of the other major industrial countries have become enormously talented at playing their own game within the larger overall rules established by the United States. However, a real change in the working of the system will come only when the United States is forced to make basic policy changes to suit the agenda of its partners as well as the other way around.

Japan

If for the United States, the problem was that the need for change was unrecognized, in the case of Japan change was undesired. Japan's adaptation to the international economic environment established by the United States has been unrivalled in its success. Having the United States play the role of supreme economic, political and military power has not prevented Japan from becoming the world's most potent industrial country and its largest investor of foreign capital. In the spring of 1987, Japan's net international assets reached $180 billion (while the American net international debt was soaring to $200 billion.)[9] The present Japanese elite, in business and government, has steered its country to unimagined gains. Nothing could be more unwelcome to the Japanese than the notion of accepting the drastically altered role that their economic prowess appears to be forcing on them. Yet the odds are that Japanese policies will change. What will cause Japan to move is that its strategy of the past four decades has run its course. Two things now imperil Japan's future economic progress — the snail's pace of growth in the international economy that has become the fate of all industrial countries under America's limping leadership; and the clear signal that Japan can push its export-led economy no further.

To date, Japan's response to the chorus of criticisms of its trade policies has broken no new ground. The Japanese have pledged to cut their current account surplus as a proportion of GDP. The government in Tokyo has talked about modest increases in public spending, and tax cuts to stimulate domestic demand and thereby to stimulate imports. Japanese leaders have promised to scold the public and private sectors into importing more American microchips. But all this has been *pro forma*, amounting to little more than a public relations campaign to deflect international criticism of Japan. The old game continues to be played by Japan and there is no clear sign that a new one is being considered.

What is likely to force a change, however, is the way Japan's extraordinary new wealth is causing its global economic role to shift. Until now, people have thought of Japan as a great economic engine that has been flooding the world with high quality manufactured products, automobiles, computers, television sets and VCRs, to name some of the most important. Now, however, as the Yen has soared and the dollar has fallen (in May 1987, the dollar was worth 143 Yen, down from 255 in the fall of 1985), Japan's capital exports have been growing mightily. This capital has been flowing into other countries in the form of indirect and direct investments. Indirect investments have gone into bonds and stocks where ownership was not being acquired. Direct investments have gone into the takeover of foreign firms and the establishment from scratch of Japanese branch plants. It will not be long before the character of Japanese trade is fundamentally altered by this process. In many cases, instead of simply exporting a manufactured product, Japanese subsidiaries in other countries will import know-how, capital equipment and parts and components from their head offices in Japan and will then carry out final assembly abroad. Such subsidiaries will create jobs abroad and will deflect political criticism of Japan's exporting practices, which will have taken a new and less visible form. Japan itself will specialize more in high- value manufacturing and in banking and services, becoming the headquarters for global economic operations. This evolution will make it much harder for other countries to mount protectionist campaigns against Japan and will also make Japan's economic fortunes much more dependent on the well-being of the global economy. Leading the move to establish foreign subsidiaries have been auto companies such as Toyota, Honda and Nissan. Japanese banks, now the world's largest, have been moving into the United States, buying up American banks and in the process acquiring know- how for dealing with the American market. In the past couple of years, Mitsubishi Bank bought the Bank of California; Fuji Bank took over the Chicago finance firm of Walter E. Heller; Sumitomo acquired a $500 million stake in Goldman Sachs; and Nippon Life Insurance bought a 13 per cent interest in Shearson Lehman Brothers for $538 million — to cite a few examples.[10]

It is this transition, now well underway, which will force Japan to play a leadership role in the global economy. Many Americans, as well as people in other parts of the world, will find themselves living in the economic hinterland of the new Japan.

Western Europe

In the thirty years since the European Common Market was launched, Western Europe has fulfilled a part of its economic promise. The real income of those living in the common market countries has risen much faster than has the income of Americans. The European Community (EC) now has the world's biggest single market. Its industries have almost closed the productivity gap with American industry and, in significant cases, such as West Germany's production of machinery, they have proven themselves to be the world's best. In a range of fields — Italian industrial design, French high speed trains, Western European aircraft — the EC is state of the art. The EC today is more than the sum of its parts, more than simply an aggregate of its member's national economies. National sovereignty and national economic initiative have remained paramount, it is true, but with the EC Western Europe has been moving toward a more integrated economic and political destiny. To put the movement into perspective, let us briefly review the steps toward integration that have been taken since the war.

Under the inspiration of Jean Monnet, who was the personality behind the Plan in France, the Council of Europe was established in 1949, and in 1951 Monnet also fostered the creation of the European Coal and Steel Community (ECSC).[11] The EEC (European Economic Community) itself was established through the Treaty of Rome in 1957 and it was under the auspices of the EEC that the common market was launched, (eliminating duties between member countries over a ten-year transitional period), and that the Common Agricultural Policy (CAP) was established. (Originally the EEC had six members and these were joined by Britain, Ireland, and Denmark which became definitive members after a five year transition in 1978. Since then, Greece, Spain and Portugal have become members. At present Austria, Norway, Turkey and Malta are applying, or are considering applying for membership.) In principle at least, the EEC is moving toward a common market without economic frontiers by 1992. An important integrative step came in the late 1970s with the direct election of the European Parliament, which sits in Strasbourg, France.

Assessing the impact of the EEC is no easy task. Much of the tariff reduction and much of the political cooperation that has occurred over the past several decades could have been expected in any event, in a Western Europe closely allied with the United States and determined to stay out of the Soviet bloc. Measuring the economic impact of the common market has given rise to controversies among analysts who have studied it using different methodologies. A number of studies have estimated that the amount of trade created as a result of the common market in 1970 was $10 billion and that the amount of trade diverted as a result of the existence of the market was $1 billion. If correct, this represented a gain of nearly 2 per cent of the EEC's GDP.[12]

Italy gained significantly in industrial strength vis-à- vis northern Europe after joining the common market, while, on the other hand, Britain continued its industrial decline after becoming a member. To what extent common market membership was responsible for these different outcomes is difficult to say, considering that the two countries were pursuing quite different economic policies. One important study made on the Cambridge Policy Group's econometric model concluded that membership in the common market had resulted in a significant loss to British industry and to British national income. A counter-study disputed the result and postulated a modest net export gain for Britain as a result of joining the common market.[13]

Over the long term, the European Community has been changing the economic context in which Western Europe countries operate. The European Court of Justice has been gaining authority to strike down laws in member countries which have placed impediments in the way of intra-market trade. While most industrial policy making still occurs in a national context in Western Europe, there have been significant examples of larger cooperation, one of which, as noted, has been the growth of Airbus. Another example has been a willingness throughout Western Europe to consider the creation of a continental rail system of high-speed trains modelled on the French TGV.

If Europe's achievements are there to be seen, so are its major problems — the leading one being massive long-term unemployment. In the spring of 1987, the unemployment rates in the major Western European countries were as follows: Italy 14.7 per cent; France 11.1 per cent; Britain 10.9 per cent; and West Germany 8.9 per cent.[14] West Germany's extremely cautious economic policies have played a significant role in this slow pace of continental economic growth. By holding its inflation rate down to nearly zero and refusing to reflate its domestic economy, the West German government has made it difficult for the rest of the EC to reflate without suffering the fate that befell the Socialist regime in France in the early 1980s.

By the 1980s, West Germany, like Japan, had reached a point where its export-led economy could no longer deliver the rapid growth needed to bring its unemployment rates down to acceptable levels. In the meantime, the whole European Community was marching at a reduced pace. In the case of Western Europe, a new political initiative appears to be needed to undertake the reflation of the economy on a continental scale. While the political inspiration for this could originate from elsewhere, serious action requires West German participation.

The Road Ahead

In this summary of how things stand in the golden triad, the barriers to change appear large — if anything, too large. Any cataloguing of the forces of the status quo tends to make it seem that change can never come. It is not unlikely that it will take a sharpening of the crisis in the major industrial economies, perhaps a new recession, to open the doors to a rebuilding of the structure of the global economy. Even a recession would bring with it no guarantee of sharpened thought, of course.

There is good reason to believe that the present arrangements for the global economy cannot endure much longer. The game that has been played in the 1980s can be described as one of "competitive deflation," to use the phrase of Cambridge economist Ajit Singh.[15] It has been a game in which the successful industrial powers have competed to cut their costs to the bone to gain access to the great American market. Much of the growth that came in the wake of the 1981-82 recession was achieved this way. But the United States is no longer strong enough to sustain the game, and the other industrial economies are now paying the price for American economic weakness. If satisfactory growth is to be resumed, the relationships among the major industrial economies can no longer focus on the United States as the centre of the system, a centre whose bounties are supposed to keep everything afloat. How is the game of competitive deflation likely to be replaced?

There have been plenty of proposals for keeping the present system afloat a little longer. The most popular one has been to encourage the United States to reduce its government deficit and its need for foreign capital by raising taxes at the same time as Japan and West Germany undertake significant reflation of their economies to take up the slack in global demand. While such a series of coordinated steps might help keep things going a little longer, they add up in the end to only tinkering with a system that is in chaos.

Beyond such recipes for keeping the present order intact, there appear to be two broad alternative possibilities for the future: the reform of the system, or more or less serious disintegration within it. Reform would mean a reordering of the global economic system to establish new mechanisms for a general reflation, for managing currency exchange rates in an orderly fashion, for making credit available to those in a deficit position. To work, a new beginning, as basic as that made at the end of the war at Bretton Woods, would have to be undertaken to trust the fate of the major industrial countries to a new and broadened leadership. The principles of such a new beginning would almost certainly have to draw upon the insights that have been gained in the development of the enterprise- intervention economies.

There is no guarantee that such a fundamental reordering of the global economy will be undertaken. The alternative may be that the golden triad disintegrates into its constituent parts — a more Asia-centred Japan; a powerful, but inward-focussed Western Europe, and an America still dominating those considerable sections of the global economy where its investments hold sway.

Whichever of these alternatives is taken, the world is likely to be a very different place in the year 2000, one in which the living standards of people in Japan and the leading countries of Western Europe will be higher than those in any of the English-speaking countries, including the United States.

Appendix

Table 1
Real Gross Domestic Product
(Year to year percentage changes)

	Average					
	50-60	60-68	68-73	73-79	79-84	50-84
United States	3.3	4.5	3.3	2.6	2.0	3.3
Japan	8.8	10.4	8.4	3.6	3.9	7.8
West Germany	8.0	4.1	4.9	2.3	0.9	4.6
France	4.6	5.4	5.9	3.1	1.1	4.2
Britain	2.7	3.1	3.2	1.5	0.6	2.4
Italy	5.5	5.7	4.6	2.6	1.2	4.3
Canada	n/a	5.6	5.6	3.4	1.7	4.2[1]

1 For the period 1960-84.
Source: OECD, *Historical Statistics 1960-1984*, p.44; and *The Economist, Economic Statistics 1900-1983*, p.127

Table 2
Real Gross Domestic Product Per Person Employed
(Year to year percentage changes)

	Average				
	60-68	68-73	73-79	79-84	60-84
United States	2.6	1.2	0.2	0.7	1.3
Japan	8.8	7.3	.2.9	2.9	5.8
West Germany	4.2	4.1	2.9	1.5	3.3
France	4.9	4.7	2.8	1.4	3.6
Britain	2.7	3.0	1.3	1.7	2.2
Italy	6.3	4.9	1.7	0.7	3.7
Canada	2.7	2.7	0.5	0.6	1.7

Source: OECD, *Historical Statistics 1960-1984*, p.47

Table 3
Real Value Added in Manufacturing
(Year to year percentage changes)

	Average				
	60-68	68-73	73-79	79-84	60-84
United States	5.6	3.9	2.0	...	3.3
Japan	13.5	12.7	3.6	7.7	9.6
West Germany	5.0	5.5	1.7	0.2	3.2
France	7.4	8.1	3.0	0.3	4.9
Britain	3.1	2.9	-0.7	-1.7	1.1
Italy	8.0	6.1	3.1	0.8	4.8
Canada	6.8	6.2	2.7	-0.1	4.1

Source: OECD, *Historical Statistics 1960-1984*, p.46

Table 4
Gross Domestic Product Per Head At Constant Prices

	Britain	United States	France	West Germany	Italy	Japan
	Pounds 1980	Dollar 1972	Franc 1985	DM 1975	L'000 1975	Y'000 1975
1950	1,888	3,511	10,624	5,741	793.7	207.6
1980	3,555	6,377	31,761	19,578	2,697.9	1,719.6

Source: *The Economist, Economic Statistics 1900-1983*, p.129

Table 5
Stock of Industrial Robots in 1983:
Selected Countries

Country	Number of Units
Japan	16,500
U.S.	8,000
West Germany	4,800
Sweden	1,900
Italy	1,800
Britain	1,753
France	1,500

Robots Per 10,000 Employed in Manufacturing

	1974	1978	1980	1981
Japan	1.9	4.2	8.3	13.0
U.S.	0.8	2.1	3.1	4.0
Sweden	1.3	13.2	18.7	29.9
West Germany	0.4	0.9	2.3	4.6
Britain	0.1	0.2	0.6	1.2
France	0.1	0.2	1.1	1.9

Source: OECD, *Productivity in Industry*, Paris, 1986, p. 105.

Table 6

Japanese Production of "High-Tech" Products

	Semi-Conductor Devices	Integrated Circuits	*Yen(Billion)* Industrial Robots	Copying Machines	Tele-communications Equipment
1970	100	53	---	40	--
1975	222	118	2	113	401
1978	251	281	6	232	504
1980	294	570	14	337	602
1981	378	689	26	421	705
1982	360	835	42	415	801
1983	421	1140	57	492	938

Source: OECD, *Japan*, Paris 1985, p. 74.

Table 7

Output Per Head, Cars and Commercial Vehicles

	Britain	U.S.	France	West Germany	Italy	Japan
1960	0.0346	0.0369	0.0300	0.0385	0.0133	0.0052
1980	0.0235	0.0281	0.0741	0.0625	0.0285	0.0943

Source: *The Economist, Economic Statistics, 1900-1983*, p. 129.

Table 8
Military Expenditures in Constant 1982 Dollars
1975 - 1983
(millions of dollars)

	1975	1983	Per Capita dollars		Percent of GNP	
			1980	1983	1980	1983
United States	150,427	208,337	736	888	5.5	6.6
Canada	4,697	6,177	225	248	1.9	2.2
France	17,274	22,827	398	417	4.0	4.2
W.Germany	20,412	22,608	353	367	3.3	3.4
Italy	7,098	9,219	146	162	2.4	2.7
Japan	6,916	11,034	80	92	0.9	1.0
Soviet Union[1]	207,426	247,525	878	908	14.1	14.0
Sweden	3,024	3,197	368	385	3.1	3.3

[1] U.S. estimate

Source: U.S. Department of Commerce, *Statistical Abstract of the United States, 1986*, p. 862

Notes

Introduction:

[1] *International Herald Tribune*, September 5, 1986.
[2] *Ibid.*, November 7, 1986.
[3] *Ibid.*, November 24, 1986.
[4] *Ibid.*, November 24, 1986.
[5] *Ibid.*, September 5, 1986.
[6] Compiled from OECD, *Historical Statistics 1960-1984*, (Paris, 1986).
[7] *Ibid.*
[8] *International Herald Tribune*, July 19, 1986.
[9] OECD, *op. cit.*
[10] *Ibid.*, and *The Economist*, October 25, 1986.
[11] *Ibid.*

Chapter 1:

[1] David A. Stockman, *The Triumph of Politics* , (Coronet Books, 1986).
[2] *Ibid.*, pp. 83-105.
[3] *Ibid.*, p. 104.
[4] *Ibid.*, pp. 107-143.
[5] OECD, *United States*, (Paris, 1986), p. 23.
[6] *Ibid.*, pp. 26, 27.
[7] *Ibid.*, p. 26.
[8] *Ibid.*, p. 134.
[9] OECD, *Historical Statistics*, p. 41.
[10] OECD, *United States*, p. 134.
[11] *Ibid.*, p. 15.
[12] *International Herald Tribune*, January 6, 1987.
[13] *Ibid.*, January 6, 1987.
[14] *Ibid.*, January 6, 1987.
[15] *Ibid.*, January 6, 1987.
[16] *Ibid.*, July 19, 1986.
[17] *Ibid.*, July 19, 1986.

[18] OECD, *United States*, p. 46.
[19] *Ibid.*, p. 46.
[20] *The Economist*, January 10, 1987.
[21] OECD, *United States*, p. 107.
[22] *Ibid.*, p. 107.
[23] *Ibid.*, p. 105.
[24] *Ibid.*, p. 105.
[25] *New York Times*, April 30, 1985.
[26] OECD, *United States* , p. 113.
[27] OECD, *Historical Statistics*, p. 44.
[28] *Ibid.*, p. 44.
[29] *The Economist*, January 31, 1987.
[30] OECD, *Historical Statistics*, p. 45.
[31] *Ibid.*, pp. 45, 46.
[32] *Ibid.*, p. 46.
[33] *Ibid.*, p. 47.
[34] *Ibid.*, p. 48.
[35] *Ibid.*, p. 49.
[36] *Ibid.*, p. 47.
[37] OECD, *United States*, p. 12.
[38] *Ibid.*, p. 13, and *The Economist*, January 31, 1987.
[39] OECD, *United States*, p. 13.
[40] *Ibid.*, p. 66.
[41] *Ibid.*, p. 62.
[42] *Ibid.*, p. 113.
[43] *Ibid.*, p. 115.
[44] *Ibid.*, p. 19.

Chapter 2:

[1] Daniel J. Boorstin, *The Americans: The Colonial Experience*, (Vintage, 1958), p. 105.
[2] Daniel J. Boorstin, *The Americans: The National Experience*, (Vintage, 1965), p. 65.
[3] *Ibid.*, pp. 116-119.
[4] *Ibid.*, p. 33.
[5] Robert B. Reich, *The Next American Frontier*, (Times Books, 1983), pp. 64-66.
[6] As cited in Daniel J. Boorstin, *The Americans: The Democratic Experience*, (Vintage, 1974), p. 363.
[7] *The Economist, Economic Statistics, 1900-1983*, p. 127.
[8] *Ibid.*, p. 127.

[9]Robert H. Hayes and William J. Abernathy, "Managing Our Way to Economic Decline," *Survival Strategies for American Industry*, (*Harvard Business Review*, 1983), p. 28.

[10] Department of Commerce, *Statistical Abstract of the United States 1986*, p. 331.

[11] *Ibid.*, p. 332.

[12] *Ibid.*, p. 581.

[13] *Ibid.*, pp. 578, 579.

[14] *Ibid.*, p. 333.

Chapter 3:

[1] Keith Smith, *The British Economic Crisis*, (Pelican, 1984), p. 68.

[2] *Ibid.*, p. 69.

[3] Anthony Sampson, *The Changing Anatomy of Britain*, (Coronet, 1983), p. 365.

[4] *Ibid.*, p. 61.

[5] Smith, *op. cit.*, pp. 80, 81.

[6] OECD, *United Kingdom*, (Paris, 1986), p. 65.

[7] Smith, *op. cit.*, p. 35.

[8] Sampson, *op. cit.*, 52.

[9] *The Economist, Economic Statistics*, p. 16 and p. 26.

[10] U.S. Department of Commerce, *Statistical Abstract of the United States, 1986*, p. 862.

[11] Smith, *op. cit.*, p. 91.

[12] *Ibid.*, p. 247.

[13] *The Economist*, May 23, 1987.

[14] *International Herald Tribune*, June 15, 1987.

Chapter 4:

[1] Ryoshin Minami, *The Economic Development of Japan: A Quantitative Study*, (Macmillan, 1986), p. 19.

[2] *Ibid.*

[3] Yoshihara Kunio, *Japanese Economic Development*, (Oxford, 1986), p. 51.

[4] *Ibid.*, pp. 52, 53.

[5] *Ibid.*, p. 15.

[6] *Ibid.*, pp. 52, 53.

[7] *Ibid.*, p. 15.

[8] *Ibid.*, p. 20.

[9] *Ibid.*, p. 20.

[10] *Ibid.*, p. 126.

[11] *Ibid.*, pp. 161-163.

[12] As cited in Keith Smith, *The British Economic Crisis*, p. 221.

[13] *Ibid.*, p. 220.
[14] Kunio, *op. cit.*, pp. 160, 161.
[15] Yutaka Kosai and Yoshitaro Ogino, *The Contemporary Japanese Economy*, (Macmillan, 1984), p. 127.
[16] *The Economist, Economic Statistics 1900-1983*, p. 120.
[17] Kunio, *op. cit.*, p. 25.
[18] OECD, *Japan*, (Paris, 1985), p. 73.
[19] Ibid., p. 75.
[20] *Ibid.*, p. 74.
[21] *Ibid.*, p. 68.
[22] *Ibid.*, pp. 56 and 72.
[23] *Ibid.*, p. 73.
[24] *Ibid.*, p. 77.
[25] OECD, *Productivity in Industry*, (Paris, 1986), p. 105.
[26] *Ibid.*, p. 33.
[27] OECD, *Japan*, p. 75.
[28] *International Herald Tribune*, January 5, 1987.
[29] *Ibid.*, January 5, 1987.
[30] *Ibid.*, January 5, 1987.
[31] Kunio, *op. cit.*, pp. 144, 145.
[32] *Ibid.*, p. 145.
[33] *International Herald Tribune*, November 7, 1986.
[34] *Ibid.*, November 7, 1986.
[35] *The Economist*, February 14, 1987. The study will be published under the title, *Flexibility: the Next Competitive Battle*, by A. de Neyer, F. Ferdows, J. Miller, A. Roth, and J. Nakane.
[36] *The Economist, Economic Statistics 1900-1983*, p. 127.
[37] *Ibid.*, p. 120.
[38] OECD, *Japan*, pp. 114, 116, 117.
[39] *The Economist*, February 21, 1987.
[40] *Ibid.*, February 21, 1987.

Chapter 5:

[1] V.R. Berghahn, *Modern Germany*, (Cambridge Press, 1982), p. 205.
[2] *Ibid.*, p. 206.
[3] *Ibid.*, p. 206.
[4] Klaus Hinrich Hennings, "West Germany," in Andrea Boltho (ed.), *The European Economy: Growth and Crisis*, (Oxford, 1982), p. 480.
[5] *Ibid.*, pp. 479, 480.
[6] *Ibid.*, p. 480.
[7] OECD, *Historical Statistics*, p. 67.
[8] Hennings, *op. cit.*, p. 481.
[9] *Ibid.*, p. 481.

[10] Willi Semmler, "Economic Aspects of Model Germany: A Comparison with the United States," in Andrei S. Markovits (ed.), *The Political Economy of West Germany*, (Praeger, 1982), p. 28.

[11] Hennings, *op. cit.*, p. 484.

[12] Semmler, *op. cit.*, p. 28.

[13] Hennings, *op. cit.*, p. 483.

[14] OECD, *Historical Statistics 1960-1984*, p. 44.

[15] *The Economist, Economic Statistics*, p. 92.

[16] Hennings, *op. cit.*, p. 485.

[17] *Ibid.*, p. 481.

[18] OECD, Historical Statistics 1960-1984, p. 44.

[19] OECD, *Germany* , (Paris, 1986), p. 86.

[20] OECD, *Historical Statistics 1960 - 1984*, p. 44.

[21] *Ibid.*, p. 47.

[22] *Ibid.*, p. 44.

[23] *Ibid.*, p. 39 and *The Economist*, June 6, 1987.

[24] OECD, *Germany*, p. 8.

[25] Andrew P. Black, "Industrial Policy in West Germany. Policy in Search of a Goal?", in Graham Hall (ed.), *European Industrial Policy*, (Croom Helm, 1986), pp. 94, 95.

[26] OECD, *Germany*, p. 79.

[27] Black, *op. cit.*, p. 97.

[28] *International Herald Tribune*, September 1, 1986, and *The Economist*, January 3, 1987.

[29] OECD, *Productivity in Industry*, p. 105.

[30] *Ibid.*, pp. 80-93.

[31] Black, *op. cit.*, p. 100.

[32] *Ibid.*, p. 101.

[33] *Ibid.*, p. 103.

Chapter 6:

[1] OECD, *France*, (Paris, 1986), p. 18.

[2] John Ardagh, *The New France*, (Penguin, 1977), p. 31.

[3] John Ardagh, *France in the 1980s*, (Pelican, 1982), p. 34.

[4] Michel Ozenda and Dominique Strauss-Kahn, "French planning: decline or renewal?," in Howard Machin and Vincent Wright (eds.), *Economic Policy and Policy-Making under the Mitterand Presidency 1981-1984*, (Frances Pinter, 1985), p. 102.

[5] Ozenda and Strauss-Kahn, *op. cit.*, p. 102.

[6] OECD, *Historical Statistics 1960-1984*, p. 44.

[7] OECD, *Productivity in Industry*, p. 14.

[8] OECD, *Historical Statistics 1960-1984*, p. 44.

[9] OECD, *Productivity in Industry*, p. 87.

[10] OECD, *Historical Statistics 1960-1984*, p. 39.

[11] *The Economist, Economic Statistics 1900-1983*, p. 80.

[12] Howard Machin and Vincent Wright, "Economic Policy under the Mitterand Presidency, 1981-1984: an introduction," in Machin and Wright (eds.), *op. cit.*, p. 1.

[13] See Janice McCormick, "Apprenticeship for governing: an assessment of French Socialism in power," in Machin and Wright (eds.), *op. cit* ., pp. 44-62.

[14] OECD, *Historical Statistics 1960-1984*, p. 83.

[15] Christian Stoffaes, "The Nationalizations: an initial assessment, 1981-1984," in Machin and Wright, p. 144.

[16] Ardagh, *The New France* , p. 38.

[17] Machin and Wright, "Economic policy under the Mitterand Presidency, 1981-1984," p. 22.

[18] Stoffaes, "The Nationalizations: an initial assessment, 1981-1984," in Machin and Wright, p. 159.

[19] OECD, *Historical Statistics 1960-1984*, p. 39.

[20] *The Economist*, May 2, 1987.

[21] OECD, *Historical Statistics 1960-1984*, p. 63.

Chapter 7:

[1] *International Herald Tribune*, March 5, 1987.

[2] OECD, *Historical Statistics 1960-1984*, p. 44.

[3] *The Economist, Economic Statistics 1900-1983*, pp. 130, 132.

[4] *Ibid.*, p. 128.

[5] *Ibid.*, p. 101.

[6] Guido Rey, "Italy," in Andrea Boltho (ed.), *The European Economy*, p. 506.

[7] *Ibid.*, p. 512.

[8] *Ibid.*, pp. 512, 513.

[9] *Ibid.*, p. 505 and OECD, *Historical Statistics 1960-1984*, p. 44.

[10] *The Economist, op. cit* ., p. 107.

[11] OECD, *Historical Statistics 1960-1984*, p. 44.

[12] *Ibid.*, p. 45.

[13] *The Economist, op. cit.*, p. 101.

[14] OECD, *Historical Statistics 1960-1984*, p. 19.

[15] *Ibid.*, p. 48.

[16] *Ibid.*, p. 83.

[17] *Ibid.*, p. 83 and OECD, *Italy*, (Paris, 1985), p. 9 and *The Economist*, February 28, 1987.

[18] OECD, *Historical Statistics 1960-1984*, p. 44.

[19] *Ibid.*, p. 44.

[20] *Ibid.*, p. 44 and OECD, *Italy*, p. 9 and *The Economist*, February 28, 1987.

[21] OECD, *Italy*, p. 80.

[22] *International Herald Tribune*, December 3, 1986.

[23] Alfredo Del Monte, "The Impact of Italian Industrial Policy 1960-1980," in Graham Hall (ed.), *European Industrial Policy*, p. 129.

[24] Henry Parris, Pierre Pestieau and Peter Saynor, *Public Enterprise in Western Europe*, (Croom Helm, 1987), p. 184.

[25] *Ibid.*, p. 42.

[26] William Nicol and Douglas Yuill, "Regional Problems and Policy," in Andrea Boltho (ed.), *op. cit.*, p. 433.

[27] Alfredo Del Monte, *op. cit.*, pp. 136- 138.

[28] Nicol and Yuill, *op. cit.*, p. 417.

[29] *Ibid.*, p. 417.

[30] *Ibid.*, p. 417.

[31] OECD, *Italy*, p. 36.

[32] Del Monte, *op. cit.*, p. 131.

[33] *International Herald Tribune*, December 3, 1986.

[34] Del Monte, *op. cit*, pp. 146, 147.

[35] *Ibid.*, p. 130.

[36] *International Herald Tribune*, December 3, 1986.

[37] *Ibid.*, December 3, 1986.

Chapter 8:

[1] OECD, *Sweden*, (Paris, 1985), pp. 38, 39.

[2] OECD, *Productivity in Industry*, p. 105.

[3] Palle Schelde Andersen and Johnny Akerholm, "Scandinavia," in Andrea Boltho (ed.), *op. cit.*, p. 618.

[4] *Ibid.*, p. 610, and *The Economist, Economic Statistics 1900-1983*, p. 127.

[5] Andersen and Akerholm, *op. cit.*, p. 626.

[6] *Ibid.*, and *The Economist, op. cit.*, p. 127.

[7] *The Economist*, March 7, 1987.

[8] OECD, *Sweden*, pp. 47, 48.

[9] *Ibid.*, p. 41.

[10] *Ibid.*, p. 42.

[11] *The Economist*, March 7, 1987.

[12] OECD, *Sweden*, p. 43.

[13] Swedish Institute, *General Facts on Sweden*, February 1983.

[14] Swedish Institute, *Labour Relations in Sweden*, March 1984.

[15] *The Economist*, March 7, 1987.

[16] *Ibid.*, March 7, 1987.

[17] *Ibid.*, March 7, 1987.

[18] Parris, Pestieau and Saynor, *op. cit.*, p. 188.

[19] *The Economist*, February 21, 1987.